free derry wall

Jim Collins & Adrian Kerr

GUILDHALL PRESS

First published in November 2009

GUILDHALL PRESS
Unit 15, Ráth Mór Business Park
Bligh's Lane
Creggan
Derry
Ireland
BT48 0LZ

T: 00 44 28 7136 4413
E: info@ghpress.com
W: www.ghpress.com

The authors/photographers assert their moral rights in this work in accordance with the Copyright, Designs and Patents Act 1998.

All photographs © Jim Collins unless otherwise attributed.

Cover and inside design by Denise Meenan
Copyright © Jim Collins/Adrian Kerr/Guildhall Press
www.freederrywall.com
ISBN: 978 1 906271 23 7

A CIP record for this book is available from the British Library.

Guildhall Press gratefully acknowledges the financial support of the Arts Council of Northern Ireland as a principal funder under its Annual Support for Organisations Programme.

Guildhall Press is grateful to Derry City Council for Service Level Agreement support under the remit of the Heritage and Museum Service.

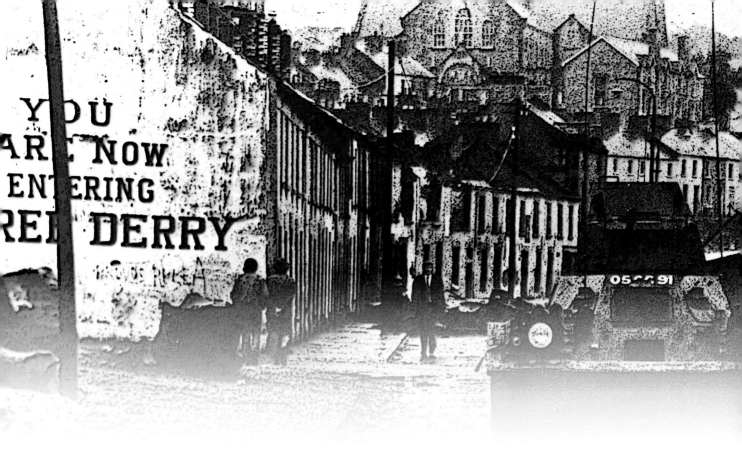

acknowledgements

Our thanks go to all those who helped in the production of this book by giving permission for their photographs to be used, or by writing contributions, including the many that were sacrificed due to lack of space.

Special thanks to Denise Meenan for her wonderful design work, and to Colm Barton who was one of the founding members of this project many, many years ago. Thanks also to Sharon Meenan, Sarah McCloskey, John Gallagher, Dorothy, Spassy McGilloway and the McKane family.

We have attempted to accredit all photographs where possible. If we have missed any, please accept our apologies and notify us in the event of any reprints. Our thanks to the following photographers: Jim Collins, Jarlath Kearney, Charlie McMenamin, Dave Mitchell, Hugh Gallagher, Frankie McMenamin, Stephen Gargan, Laurie Sparham, John McKane, Peter O'Kane, Jim Davies, Frank Middlebrook, Jim Keys, Ronan Moyne, Clive Limpkin, Joe Campbell, Adrian Kerr, Declan McLaughlin, Barney McMonagle, Eamon Melaugh, Ciarán Ó Dochartaigh, George Sweeney, Willie Carson Collection, *Derry Journal*, AP/RN, Camerawork, the CAIN website (www.cain.ulst.ac.uk) and Guildhall Press. Thanks also to the *Derry News* for permission to use extracts from some of their reports.

Our appreciation also goes to Declan Carlin, Joe McAllister, Jenni Doherty, John Bryson, Kevin and Paul Hippsley at Guildhall Press.

about the authors

An artist from the Bogside, **Jim Collins** has had a long association with Free Derry Wall. Since the early 1980s, Jim has initiated and collaborated on arts projects, utilising the front and the back of the Wall to promote debate and dialogue on local and international issues. Jim is currently researching a publication on Derry's Rossville Flats. The project will explore the everyday lives of residents from the high-rise flat complex that has borne witness to much of Derry's recent turbulent history. If you wish to contribute to this project contact: hawksrossville@hotmail.com

Adrian Kerr is co-editor of *Perceptions: Cultures in Conflict* (Guildhall Press, 1996) and *No Go: A Photographic Record of Free Derry* (Guildhall Press, 1997), and has edited and/or contributed to a number of other publications on the recent history of Derry. He is the manager of the Museum of Free Derry, the Bloody Sunday Trust-sponsored museum set up to tell the story of the civil rights and Free Derry era from the point of view of the Free Derry community. See www.museumoffreederry.org for further information on the museum.

contents

We have listed a few of the main articles to give a flavour of the contributions.

introduction

The words 'You Are Now Entering Free Derry' were first handwritten on the gable wall of a derelict house in Derry's Lecky Road on 5 January 1969. The reasons and background to this are explained within. The location soon became known as Free Derry Wall (also referred to as Free Derry Corner) and a focal point for the many tumultuous events that occurred in the city in the ensuing decades. These events attracted international media attention and gained global recognition for the Wall and its defiant message.

The idea of capturing and telling the story of the Wall first emerged around the thirtieth anniversary of its creation, but for many reasons it has taken us somewhat longer than we envisaged to gather our thoughts and the many contributions. We are therefore pleased to bring it out in the year of the Wall's fortieth anniversary.

Over the last ten years, we approached numerous individuals for their views on Free Derry Wall, both by letter and in person, and published a number of public appeals for submissions in the media and over the internet.

The time span has allowed the range of views and images collected to reflect what has been going on around the Wall and around the world in those years, and to show how the Wall itself has echoed those events.

We received hundreds of responses and have included as many here as space allows. The contributions are unedited and all terminology and views presented are those of the individual contributors.

We wanted to explore and debate if Free Derry Wall, front and back, has developed from a hastily scrawled slogan of protest to an international icon of civil rights for all. Or is it just a piece of history, a symbol from the past, only relevant now as a tourist attraction and backdrop for photographs? Read the contributions, look at the photographs, think for a while, and make up your own mind.

Whatever you feel or decide, the story of Free Derry Wall is evolving daily. And who knows what remains to be written about, or even on, its changing facade?

Some years ago, I visited the Alamo in San Antonio, Texas. In 1836, Texas had declared itself independent of Mexico, but Mexican leader, General Antonio López de Santa Anna, was having none of it. He marched on San Antonio, took back the Alamo after a thirteen-day siege and slaughtered the 185 rebels to the man. It was a short-lived victory. The rest of Texas fought back and soon Santa Anna was captured at the Battle of San Jacinto, near Houston. Texas was on its way through a winding history which led it eventually to become one of the most important states in the Union, and the political power base of two

later that comes out in the narrative of the site. 'Remember the Alamo!' shouted the Texan soldiers at the Battle of San Jacinto as they avenged their colleagues' deaths. As the American tourists in turn remember the Alamo, do they also consider what the United States went on to do to Mexico and its neighbours in the next century and a half? Training death squads in El Salvador; funding the Contra assassins in Nicaragua; making Mexico a subordinate economy through 'free trade' agreements. That the vast majority of San Antonio's residents, and indeed the visitors to the Alamo that day, were ethnically

Presidents Bush. You can see why the Alamo is known as 'Texas' most famous shrine' and 'the cradle of Texas liberty'.

Yet the experience for me was a strange one – and I should have guessed it by the use of the word 'shrine'. There was a stark sense of solemnity in the place. People wandered around reverentially reading the plaques which gave the names of the Texans, other Americans, Scots, Irish, English and Germans who had been slaughtered. Everyone had a forename and a family name, except one: 'John, a Black Freedman'. I remarked to my companion that here was one hero who did not gain the recognition he deserved. People passing by took no time to tell me to keep quiet. I have been a tourist in noisier European cathedrals.

But there was more: although the Alamo is the scene of a Texan defeat, it is in fact the Texan victory over Mexico some months

Mexican had little effect on the way the Alamo was represented or received. Reverence was a substitute for a critical look at the history of US imperial power, a history in which the Alamo was undoubtedly a crucial turning point.

The winners write the history, they say; they also usually design the monuments and determine the story those monuments tell.

Whatever it is, the Wall at Free Derry Corner, with its famous slogan: 'You Are Now Entering Free Derry', is not a shrine, and hopefully it never will be. Spare us the protective Perspex, the all-weather roof, turnstiles, tickets, guards in uniforms and a ban on flash photography. This is a living monument because it represents a past which still resonates so strongly in everyday life in the present.

At the simplest level, the Wall represents a moment of defiance, perhaps not as grand as that at the Alamo, but in terms of Derry and indeed the North of Ireland, no less significant. It wasn't just a scrawled message on a wall; it caught the political mood of the moment. The demand for civil rights had reached a pitch and the state's response was repression. The Bogside residents were having none of it, and the rest is history. Later, the Wall witnessed so much horror, not least the massacre of Bloody Sunday. If walls could speak . . .

A lifetime after the slogan first appeared, there is hardly anyone who would not admit what everyone else in the Bogside knew then – that the demand for civil rights was a perfectly reasonable one. Even in the British state's own terms, had there been anyone there who could have recognised this point or conceded it, civil rights was perfectly reasonable. The British could have made some attempt to bring about some semblance of democracy, faced down the Unionists, and put the lid back on their client state for another generation. And that is why it has to go down in history as one of the great lost opportunities. Four decades later, it is possible to hear different groups being blamed ultimately for all the deaths and injury which occurred in the years since: if the Provos had not gone on the war path, if the Loyalists had not brought down Sunningdale, and so on. But the Wall reminds us of an underlying truth: the Brits lost the chance to deal with grievance and stood back while the Unionists tried their usual trick of bashing resistance into the ground. The Wall stands for all that. And that's why it must stand, lest we forget.

But wasn't it always like this, the short-sightedness of imperialism? Daniel O'Connell's demands for Catholic Emancipation and the Repeal of the Union were reasonable and sought by constitutional means. The British state could have taken the wind out of his sails by giving him what he sought and still held on to control of

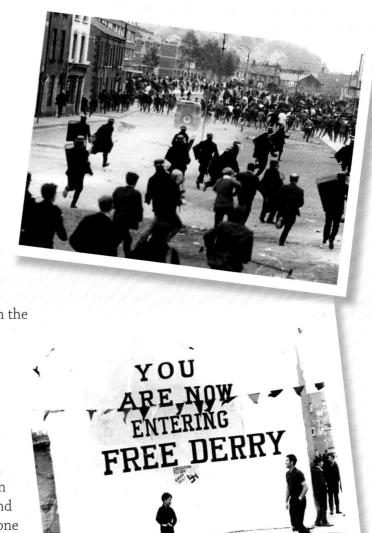

August 1969: Battle of the Bogside and the Freedom Fleadh (Barney McMonagle).

Ireland for another while. But they missed the chance. Charles Stewart Parnell's bid for Home Rule was also reasonable and constitutional, and again, could have been conceded by the British to their own benefit. Instead, the chance was missed. There is no wall at Clontarf commemorating O'Connell's monster meetings, no wall in Wicklow commemorating Parnell's challenge. But in Derry there's a wall which celebrates the challenge of civil rights and reminds us of the bloodshed which followed from the failure of the British state to concede the reasonable.

Unfortunately, by dwelling on its historical importance, I am making it sound like a shrine. But, of course, history is only part of its significance. On the back of the Wall are painted constantly changing political messages. And even the front of the Wall, arguably more sacred, has not been treated solely as a holy relic, but has been altered, sometimes dramatically, on at least half a dozen occasions. This is no museum piece, but a genuine art gallery in which the exhibits change regularly rather than being frozen for all time. The changes represent developments and debates in the community which inherited the mantle of civil rights agitation, and hence the messages of support for Palestine, women, AIDS sufferers, gay activists, East Timorese, the Birmingham Six and on and on. The struggle for equality arguably never ends; the victims change and that is the vitality of the Wall – that it can be allowed to respond to the victims.

And in a way, it is also a mirror, because sometimes the perpetrators change, too. What the messages sometimes remind us is that it is not only institutions like the British state which can create victims, but ourselves, whether it is in terms of violence against women, homophobia, racism and the like.

Finally, the wall is a call to action. Of course, Derry is not free, no more than South Africa or Guatemala. It is not as confined as it once was, or as Palestine still is. But in a sense, it has exchanged one form of bondage for others – the curse of globalisation, with its casualisation of labour, the alienation of a lot of young people, and so on. But that should never quell the aspiration for freedom from whichever bondage afflicts you. 'Free Derry' is a state of mind, a sense, however tentative, of political assurance, a confidence, even if sometimes shaky, in the collective ability of the community to argue and organise around its demands, a reminder of what people went through in order to get to where they are today. There is something almost metaphysical in what was written in 1969: 'We know where we've been, we know where we've come from, we know where we're going'.

Irish Tricolour at half-mast in 1987 (Camerawork).

In Latin America, people have a phrase which reminds them of their past while giving them the strength needed in the present. Looking back at the dictatorships in places like Chile and Guatemala, at the torture and the death squads, they say: '*Nunca mas!*' (never again).

While Free Derry Wall stands, it sends out our equivalent of the same message:

Remember Free Derry!

Bill Rolston

Above and below, 33 Lecky Road, Derry, 1969 (John McKane).

33 lecky road

No 33 Lecky Road, a small terraced house in Derry's Bogside, is in the possibly unique position of being both world famous and completely unknown. Whereas many thousands of people have gathered there over the years, and come from all over the world to be photographed against the You Are Now Entering Free Derry slogan, this address means little to anyone other than former residents of the now almost completely demolished streets.

The last recorded inhabitants of 33 Lecky Road were the McKane family, who lived in the house that was to become famous from the 1930s until the 1960s.

Lecky Road was named after the Liberal Mayor of Derry, Connolly McCausland Lecky, and opened officially in 1842. Yet the road itself followed the ancient route of Mary Blue's Burn, the remnants of a once encircling river that joined with the River Foyle, making Derry an island in medieval times. It also partially covered the line of the so-called Old Road to Strabane, so it was both a boundary road bisecting the area which became known as the Bogside and a new path from the area and city to the Letterkenny Road to the southwest. According to the Corporation, the road was named after Lecky 'as he had considerably assisted in its formation by giving up gratis certain parcels of his own private property'.

The first resident of number 33 Lecky Road we know of was a man named Thomas McCauley. He lived in the house as early as 1887 and his family were still there a decade later. By 1901, JJ McShane lived there, and the house changed hands soon after a number of times – in 1905 to Thomas Doherty, in 1909 to Mrs Rutherford,

and in 1911 to James McCourt. By 1916, John Henderson had moved in and his family lived there throughout the Tan and Civil wars. Almost directly across from the house was the Bogside Barracks of the Royal Irish (later Royal Ulster) Constabulary, and it is almost certain that local units of the Irish Republican Army opened fire from the gable of Henderson's house when they attacked the barracks in April and June of 1920.

By 1934, James McKane and his family were living at 33 Lecky Road and paying a weekly rent of 7s 5d for living in a damp house on a street that frequently flooded. Drainage repairs by the Corporation soon after rectified the flooding and pressure applied by the Derry Tenants' Defence League resulted in a rent reduction to 6s 11d and a refund of overpaid rent of 13s.

The condition of 33 Lecky Road deteriorated throughout the 1960s and the McKanes and many others departed the houses on the road around this time. This was, of course, the period of the great housing struggle by local people for more and better-quality homes at affordable rents. The Lecky Road/Hamilton Street area was a focal point for much of this agitation, including the famous incident of the Wilson family's caravan being pulled across the road and occupied by community activists in an attempt to generate media attraction for their cause.

The demolition of the houses on the north side of St Columb's Terrace and further along the Lecky Road left a large open space between the gable end of number 33 and Rossville Street. Because the area was already a hive of political activity, it was natural that meetings and street protests should continue in the vicinity of the gable end and it became a focal point. This, of

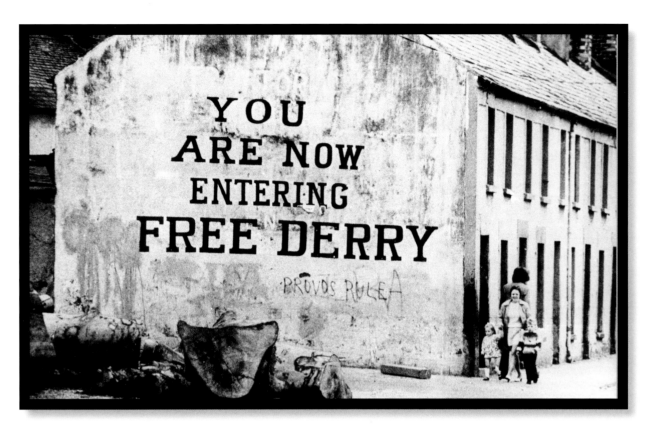

The Wall in 1970, scarred by the early days of the Troubles (Barney McMonagle).

course, was only part of a much wider tradition in Derry (and throughout urban working-class communities across the North) of street-corner gatherings where discussions, chiefly on politics and sport, held sway. Part of the great outdoor university of life, and a common sight because of the huge levels of male unemployment in Derry, these street assemblies had been discussing views and ideas, arguing and exchanging gossip, since the nineteenth century. Prior to Free Derry, Fox's Corner had probably been the nearest such meeting place, though many other locations – in St Columb's Wells, the top of Howard Street, the Little Diamond, the foot of Stanley's Walk, and the end of Cable Street – displayed a similar culture.

But it was in the early hours of 5 January 1969 that the gable end of 33 Lecky Road was to become a symbol of resistance and hope that endures to this day. Over the subsequent days and years of Free Derry – from its initial five-day flowering to the introduction of the Redcaps of the Royal Military Police and then its dismantlement after the British Army's

Operation Motorman of July 1972 – the gable end of the McKanes' old house was a magnet for an array of groupings and individuals. It was the back drop to a variety of soapboxes and activists, but always it remained a radical rendezvous for the ordinary people of Derry – their symbol of hope and freedom as well as a trenchant rejection of the orthodox sectarian political structures of the Londonderry Corporation and Stormont.

Although its position as the main gathering point for political meetings remained unchallenged in the years after Bloody Sunday and Motorman, the years were not kind to Free Derry Wall, nor indeed were those who might have been expected to be its most ardent defenders. The Wall was paint-bombed many times by the police and army, and re-painted just as often. On one occasion, it was even rammed by a Saracen armoured vehicle in an attempted demolition. At other times, both British Army officers and intelligence service personnel were keen to have their photograph taken, like so many other latter-day tourists, in front of the famous Wall. This love-hate relationship with the Wall was mirrored by the Royal Ulster Constabulary (RUC), who, between attempts at its defacement and general petty vandalism, posed late one night in the 1980s for a group photograph in front of the immortal graffiti.

The visit of Martin Galvin, the Irish-American NORAID leader, in 1989 coincided with a rally in front of Free Derry Wall to mark the twentieth anniversary of the deployment of troops here. Martin McGuinness used the occasion to call for the Wall's preservation and reminded those present of SDLP moves in 1977 to have the Wall demolished. This was a reference to comments made by Councillor Liam Bradley and the SDLP that the derelict houses remaining on the Lecky Road were dangerous to pedestrians and hazardous to passing cars. Ironically, however, it was the Derry Brigade of the IRA who, in 1975, called for the demolition of Free Derry Corner in support of claims made by Lisfannon Park residents that the shell of number 33 Lecky Road was a dangerous and insanitary building, a repository for rubbish and a breeding ground for vermin. A number of meetings later, this position changed and local Republicans switched to supporting the retention of the gable wall.

By then, the flyover, completed in December 1974 but prevented from opening by local residents until their safety concerns were satisfactorily met, had been opened and the traffic levels slowly increased. Despite this development and the continuing determination of the Housing Executive to pull down Free Derry Wall, meetings and marches continued to occur and afforded a platform for those from across the globe who wished to express solidarity with the people of Derry. By such means, the tradition of free speech, which the Wall paid homage to and encouraged, was continued and reinforced in the 1990s with the greater use of the back of the Wall to draw attention to a range of annual events and causes. Among those included were the Gasyard Féile, International Women's Day, campaigns for prisoner releases, the Gaelic language and Gay Pride.

Despite intermittent controversy over the 'control' of the back of Free Derry Wall as a result of electioneering messages being put up in recent years, the popularity of the famous landmark remains undiminished, both locally and internationally.

Máirtín Ó Catháin

Above and below, the McKane family outside their home at 33 Lecky Road (John McKane, Peter O'Kane).

"The wall was paint-bombed many times by the police and army, and re-painted just as often. On one occasion, it was even rammed by a Saracen armoured vehicle in an attempted demolition."

is it one or two r's in entering?

Who shot JFK? Where was the first moon landing really filmed? Was Shergar put out to stud in Area 51? What was Leonardo doing to make her smile like that? Who grabbed a paintbrush in the early hours of 5 January 1969 and painted the words You Are Now Entering Free Derry on the gable end of 33 Lecky Road, Bogside, Derry, Ireland?

All among the great mysteries of our age, but we can only solve them one at a time. So we should start with the most important.

The origins of the slogan You Are Now Entering Free Derry are not in dispute. Author and journalist Eamonn McCann, then one of the leaders of the civil rights uprising in Derry, 'stole' it from the free-speech campaign active around Berkeley University in California in the mid-'60s. Plagiarism at its best, and let's face it, a free-speech movement could hardly complain now, could it? During research for this book, many of those involved in that campaign were contacted and they all remember the slogan You Are Now Entering Free Berkeley, though, unfortunately, none of them could trace any photographs of it.

When the Derry version was painted is also not in doubt. On 4 January 1969, the People's Democracy march from Belfast – which had been attacked by Loyalists and off-duty B Specials all along its route and most famously and viciously at Burntollet Bridge – reached Derry. Rioting erupted as the marchers arrived in the city centre, bloodstained and battered, and the RUC and B Specials launched yet another attack on the Bogside. Lord Cameron later reported:

> With regret, our investigations have led us to the unhesitating conclusion that on the night of 4/5 January, a number of policemen were guilty of misconduct which involved assault and battery, malicious damage to property in streets in the predominantly Catholic Bogside area, giving reasonable cause for apprehension of personal injury among other innocent inhabitants, and the use of provocative sectarian and political slogans.

When that attack was repulsed, groups of mainly young people stayed around throughout the night, waiting for another attack. One of those groups was waiting at the junction of the Lecky Road and St Columb's Street and, for want of something better to do, decided on a piece of graffiti. Eamonn McCann suggested a slogan, and the rest, as they say, was criminal damage to Corporation property.

But who held the smoking paintbrush? The first published accreditation came in Eamonn McCann's *War and an Irish Town* in 1974. In it he wrote:

> John 'Caker' Casey, who by dint of his dab hand with a paintbrush was recognised as an expert wall-sloganeer, fetched out the tools of his trade and in a moment of inspiration wrote You Are Now Entering Free Derry on a gable end in St Columb's Street.

This quickly became the accepted version of events, and Caker has been widely accepted as the originator ever since, as seen in the numerous references to him throughout this book. For the rest of his life, he was associated with creating the slogan, and after his death in September 2000, a memorial stone was placed beside Free Derry Wall, praising him for his famous achievement. The graffiti 'Caker Casey was here, January 5th 1969' was painted in red on the front of the Wall on the morning following his death.

The *Derry Journal* gave Caker the following obituary under the headline 'Death of Free Derry Painter':

> One of the Bogside's best-known characters, John 'Caker' Casey – the man responsible for first daubing the famous words You Are Now Entering Free Derry on the gable end of a house at Lecky Road – died suddenly this week at his home in Dove Gardens.

The words 'Caker Casey was here, January 5th, 1969' were added on the morning after his death.

> Mr Casey (54) died on Monday at his home which, incidentally, is just yards from historic Free Derry Corner. 'Caker' was aged twenty-three in 1969 when he made his stand for freedom and painted the now world-famous slogan on a gable wall at Fox's Corner. 'You Are Now Entering Free Derry' appeared on the Wall within hours of

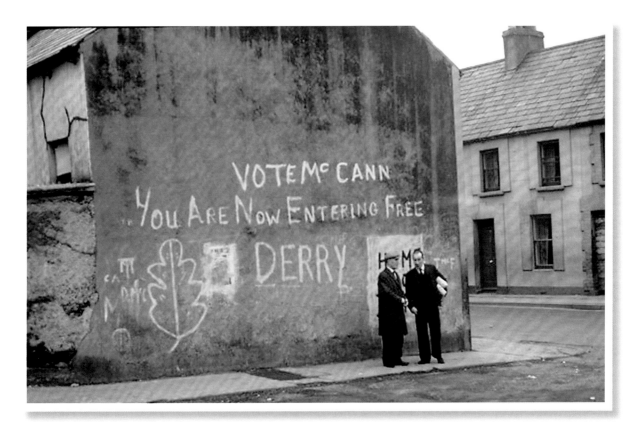

The original handwritten slogan in 1969 (Jim Davies).

a People's Democracy march – ambushed by
Loyalists at Burntollet – arriving in the city.
At 2.00am the following Sunday morning,
a group of drunken B Specials invaded the
Bogside, wreaking havoc. After a meeting of
Nationalists in Creggan Estate, a message
was relayed to the RUC, ordering them to
remove the B Specials from the Bogside or
5,000 men would force them out. The hated
Specials were quickly pulled out.

Hours later, in the general hubbub of the
Bogside, 'Caker' appeared, ladder and paint
in hand, to daub in bold, black letters the
words that would soon come to define the
northern struggle . . .

Note the *Derry Journal*'s description of the
slogan 'bold black letters' . . .

However, by this time, Eamonn McCann had
already given a different version of events,
naming a different painter of the original slogan.
In the book *A Sense of Place: Irish Lives, Irish
Landscapes*, McCann said in 2001:

It's the single most important sentence I
ever wrote . . . it was based on Berkeley.
Now, with the connotations of 'Free
Ireland', its significance seems different.
But actually, it wasn't about looking back,
it was about looking forward, looking
out towards the rest of the world. It was
a catch phrase for a cause, a slogan that
captured a particular moment at the very
start of what was to become the Troubles.
The very minute it went up, it caught on.

The article continued:

Yet for years, he [McCann] could not
remember who had actually painted the
words on the Wall for him that night in
the Bogside. Then in 1974, when he was
writing his book War and an Irish Town,
he went in search of that person. John
'Caker' Casey's name kept coming up, and
when asked by Eamonn, Caker said yes, he
could remember painting it that night. And

so he was written into history as the man
who painted You Are Now Entering Free
Derry.

For years, says Eamonn McCann, Caker
enjoyed a certain status in relation to the
Wall. He was presented with a plaque to
commemorate his involvement. His name
even appears on those tea towels.

Then about five years ago, Eamonn was
accosted by a man in a bar. 'Hey,' he said,
'I've a bone to pick with you, McCann.
It wasn't Caker who painted the Wall
that night, it was me.' Still, Eamonn had
no recollection. Until the man told him
something that jogged his memory. 'Don't
you remember, Eamonn, I was painting the
words and I came over and said to you, "Is
it one or two 'r's in entering?"'

It was that little detail that brought the
memory of it flooding back for Eamonn.
Here was Liam, the man who really
painted the Wall. Caker might have his
plaques and his name on tea towels and
the like, but he never actually painted the
slogan. 'It's like the film The Man Who
Shot Liberty Valance,' *laughs Eamonn.*
'Print the legend.'

The Liam referred to in the article was Liam
Hillen. Following one of the many published
appeals for submissions for this book, friends of
Liam contacted the authors and suggested we
talk to him. He gave us the following:

The only thing I remember from that
particular night was that there were about
sixteen of us walking around the outskirts
of the Bogside, carrying sticks and things
like that – we thought we were going to
do something about it if the Specials came
back in. I remember it was a cold night.
Somebody came back over and said to us
– I think it was Bernadette Devlin – that
the B Specials were coming back and to
come in to the Bogside. So we came in
and were standing around about Fox's

Corner. We noticed this glow from this old building and we decided to walk up. We found out it was this gutted-out house and right in the middle of it was a fire. So we walked into it and there was a whole bunch of guys all standing around this fire, just keeping themselves warm. We were standing around there, it must have been two or three in the morning, heating ourselves up, and I said to Eamonn McCann, 'Jesus, I am fed up standing

paint and a brush?' And this wee fella standing on the right-hand side of me said his aunt lived up the street a bit. So we went and found a can of yellow paint and a can of blue paint, anything else didn't have much in it. I remembered that yellow and blue made green, so I mixed them together. I got this old hard brush and me and the wee boy walked back down to the corner and up to the gable wall. Big Danny Begley was about six foot tall so he

Makeshift barricades in Rossville Street, 1984 (Camerawork).

around here doing nothing.' And Eamonn turned around and said, 'Why don't you go and paint a sign on that gable wall over there?' I asked what we should we paint up, and guys made suggestions like "We Demand Free Beer" and various other things. Then McCann turned round and said, 'Why don't you stick up "You are now entering Free Derry"?' I said, 'That's it, we'll stick that up,' and turned round and said, 'anybody know where I can get some

leaned up against the wall with his hands interlocked and gave me a lift up. Chris Armstrong held the paint and I dipped into it.

I am dyslexic, by the way – I only found that out after I had the stroke. So that's probably why I had to turn to McCann and ask him how many 'r's are in entering. And that's how McCann always remembers me.

We ended up painting it with green paint on a dirty white background. I remember watching the six o'clock news the next day and there it was: You Are Now Entering Free Derry. I can't remember after that when it was whitewashed over and painted up properly.

I never really thought about what Free Derry Corner had become until years later. I moved to England in 1974 and stayed there until 1991, and to me it had always been just a piece of graffiti, it just happened. There was no ideology thing about it, no big statement or anything like that. What we were actually doing was just declaring: 'You are now entering Free Derry, pal, and this is us, and you are not in control.' We were just metaphorically sticking two fingers up at them, saying: 'You are not coming into our territory and beating us up whenever you feel like it.' It wasn't anything intellectual . . .

So, that is Liam's version of events, supported by Eamonn McCann, Bernadette McAliskey and others who were there that night. But unfortunately, Caker is no longer around to give his version of events, and there are many who will always believe that he was the original sloganeer, and some very reliable sources who claim to have seen him paint it. Also, his accreditation as the painter could not have come out of nowhere, and he must have had some strong connection to it for the legend to have lasted for so many years. Why else did his name keep coming up when Eamonn was searching for the original painter in 1974 when he was writing *War and an Irish Town*?

But there is one piece of evidence, other than the eyewitnesses, that could go some way to resolving this. The original slogan was painted in a hurry in the middle of the night. It was a handwritten slogan, not the careful block-lettered version that has become world famous. Early film footage, such as the 1969 RTÉ programme *John Hume's Derry*, shows

the slogan in the summer of 1969 as roughly scrawled in light paint on a dark background. This contradicts the *Journal*'s description of Caker daubing the slogan in 'bold, black letters' on the gable end, but does come closer to Liam Hillen's account of lighter-coloured paint on a 'dirty, white background'. It was only after the Battle of the Bogside, in the run-up to Callaghan's visit to the Bogside, that the slogan was painted in the way it is now recognised, in the bold, black letters attributed to Caker by the *Derry Journal*.

So who *did* paint You Are Now Entering Free Derry first? If you ask me, and please don't, because I really don't have anything more to add to this, then, based on the information in this article, Liam Hillen was the man with the brush on 5 January 1969, but Caker Casey was the man with the black paint and the block letters in September 1969. Liam was the first to paint the words You Are Now Entering Free Derry; Caker was the first to paint the now famous, and familiar, lettering You Are Now Entering Free Derry. Any evidence to the contrary is welcome.

Adrian Kerr

British soldiers question the painters while the Wall receives a face-lift, 1986.

fairtheoir ar stair dhoire

Cad a chiallaíonn Free Derry Corner domh? Níor smaoinigh mé air seo ariamh. Siúlaim thar an Bhalla gach lá nach mór; is iomaí uair a d'fhreastal mé ar agóid nó ar thionól aige ach go dtí seo, ní dhearna mé machnamh ar an chiall leis. Balla mór bán? Siombal de chur in aghaidh an leatroim? Áit a mbíonn críoch le morshiúlanna Dhomhnach na Fola? Balla fógraíochta do gach saghas grúpa a bhfuil pointe le déanamh acu? Áit do thurasóirí?

Ar bhealach, tá siad sin uilig ceangailte leis an Bhalla. Ach tá níos mó ná sin sa Bhalla. Bhí Free Derry Corner mar fhairtheoir nó bhreathnadóir ar stair na coimhlinte seo ó phléasc sé i 1968. D'fhianaigh an Balla an RUC ag ionsaí St Columb's Wells i 1969 agus Cath Thaobh an Bhogaigh sa bhliain chéanna; Ár Dhomhnach na Fola, deireadh an Cheantair 'No Go', treascairt Dhealbh Walker sna seachtóidí. Sna hochtóidí, bhí an Balla ann le linn an stailc ocrais; maraíodh Stephen McConomy caoga slat ón Bhalla. Chonaic sé leagan árasán Rossville agus stad Johnny Walker ag an Bhalla tar éis dó a cheann a fháil i Sasana.

Sna nochaidí d'eitil Bratach úr na hAfraice Theas in airde ar thoghadh Mhandela mar uachtarán; chruinnigh na mílte daoine ann le tacú le muintir Bóthar Gharbhachaidh agus le héileamh na gclanna d'fhiosrúchán úr Dhomhnach na Fola. Faoi láthair, tá Bratach na bPailistíneach ag eitilt os cionn an Bhalla.

Cad a chiallaíonn sé domh? I mbeagán focal, stair agus saoirse.

Donncha Mac Niallais

Rioting in the Bogside was a daily occurrence, August 1985.

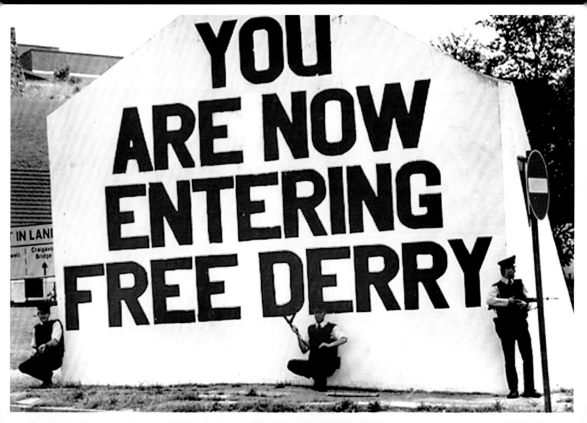

A rainbow symbol of optimism adorns the Wall on the anniversary of Bloody Sunday, 1992.

Free Derry Corner represents to me a significant symbol from the late 1960s when the ordinary people of Derry were no longer prepared to tolerate the oppression and discrimination inflicted upon them by the establishment of that time. They took to the streets in a peaceful and dignified protest against the inequalities imposed upon them for so many years.

Peaceful civil rights marches became a prominent and effective feature of that time. We felt, in our innocence, that we could correct the blatant lack of justice that had become endemic in our society. We felt that we could correct this imbalance by peaceful, disciplined protest. We marched forward with great hope, towards a better future for all of our people. We expected equal rights in housing, voting and employment.

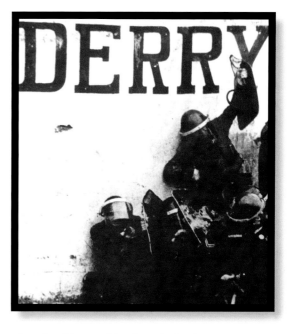

British soldiers and local youths battle for territory in the shadow of the Wall, July 1971 (Barney McMonagle).

The inadequate response from an unprepared and lethargic establishment had the inevitable consequence that our efforts towards peaceful progress were severely curtailed and gradually became much more difficult to maintain. In the absence of an adequate, sustained and visible response, increasing violence became an everyday reality.

Free Derry Corner is probably the most famous gable wall in Ireland and attracts an enormous number of tourists from the United States, from all parts of Europe, and beyond. The corner remains as a very significant tourist attraction.

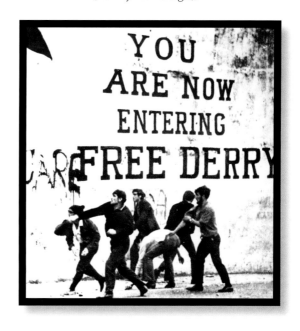

For me, the corner will always remain as a potent symbol of a courageous people, who decided as a community to discard the burden of manipulated social deprivation.

Dr Raymond McClean

View from the Bloody Sunday Monument, 1985.

British MP Ken Livingstone addresses the Bloody Sunday commemoration, 1987.

Gerry Adams addresses the Bloody Sunday rally, 1995 (Jarlath Kearney).

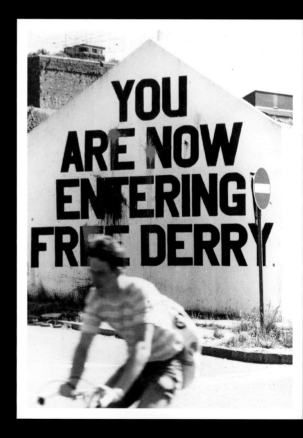

The Wall with British Army observation post on the City Walls in the background, 1986.

'You are now entering Free Derry'

The slogan is like a line from a Christian liturgy. It reminds us of what has passed and what is to come.

The gable wall is an icon which has its roots in a specific period of history. It is a landmark to the late '60s and early '70s, before the darker night of Thatcherism and Reaganism blighted our world and narrowed our vision. A time of Free Schools and Free Universities, when there was sufficient confidence amongst the people that, outrageously, they claimed the language of their oppressors and transformed it into their own. Freedom was a real song which even *we* could sing.

The gable wall linked us to the rest of the world. For throughout the world, the demand for freedom, for participatory democratic structures that genuinely empowered people, was at its height. A time of optimism, of hope, when we really did believe we could change the world and make it fit for humans to live in.

The vision remains, of course. Not as strong now as then, but still strong enough to secure its future.

Derry today is not Free. Yet the resonance of the gable wall is still with us. It points to a future that is not yet, but one day can be. Not just Free Derry, but Free Ireland, Free Europe and a Free World.

Robin Percival

Free Derry welcomes home local man Johnny Walker of the 'Birmingham 6', June 1991.

A green ribbon adorns the Wall in support of the release of political prisoners after the Good Friday Agreement in 1998. Also included are a 'sniper at work' sign and the flag of the PPK – Kurdistan Workers Party.

International Women's Day (Hugh Gallagher).

'Free Derry has given
a voice to the dispossessed
and marginalised'

Local residents welcome visiting children from the Balata refugee camp in Palestine, 2005.

Free Derry Wall for me has three aspects.

The message on the front of the Wall, You Are Now Entering Free Derry, tells the story of resistance.

Free Derry Wall is the gable wall at the bottom of St Columb's Street, the wee street where I was born and reared and where I first learned about injustice and discrimination. Where I watched my father being dragged from our home, when I was seven years old, to spend the next five years in jail without charge or trial.

What happens on the back of the Wall now has taken on much more significance than the immortalised message on the front. The back of Free Derry Wall has given a voice to the dispossessed and marginalised. It has enabled those who have been denied access to mainstream media the opportunity to bring their message to the people of Derry. And in keeping with the spirit, its symbolism and the message of the Wall, it must remain a megaphone of the people.

Roisin Barton

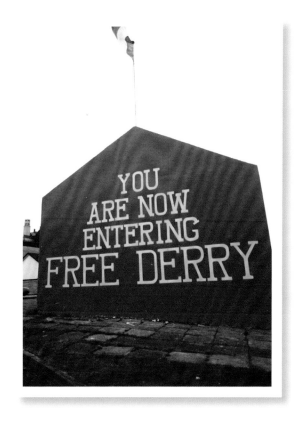

The Wall is painted red by artist Colin Darke to mark the twenty-fifth anniversary of the Battle of the Bogside, August 1994.

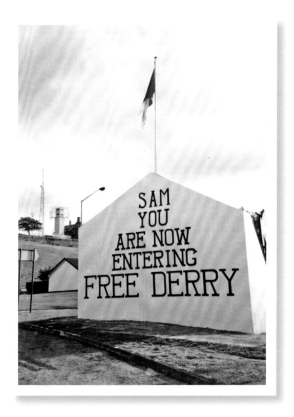

The Sam Maguire GAA trophy is welcomed to the city after Derry's All-Ireland Senior Football victory in 1993.

It was a week before Bobby Sands died on hunger strike, and the same day that I read Patrick Kinsella's *Butcher's Dozen*, that I first saw Free Derry Corner.

Looking out over the Bogside from Derry's Walls, the North's geography and that poem taught me more about Irish history than a week of reading history books.

By turning a simple wall into an international icon, the creativity and sheer determination of the people of Derry showed there's more than one way to take your message to the opposition.

Anne Cadwallader

Lecky Road, Free Derry Wall and Rossville flats can be seen in the background, 1985 (Camerawork).

Free Derry Wall was one of the first places that I visited in Derry. Every year I was honoured to be part of the commemorations for Bloody Sunday. I went to the weekend discussions and marvelled at the spirit and resilience in Derry. Free Derry Wall epitomises that spirit. I gained strength and hope and friends every time I visited Doire Colmcille and there must have been something in the air because I married a Derryman – a member of the McAteer clan. I hope that the Free Derry Corner someday becomes a reality instead of just a symbol of freedom.

Caitriona Ruane

Free Derry Corner is a symbol of how ordinary people work to overcome great unfairness in their lives. It is linked in my mind to community spirit, great ingenuity and to tales of Radio Free Derry, set up to put across a local point of view in the face of censorship of Nationalist and Republican views in the 1960s.

Bairbre de Brún

'Great ingenuity'

Martin McGuinness and Tony O'Hara at a hunger strike commemoration, 1991 (Stephen Gargan).

Free Derry Wall is a powerful symbol of resistance linking the past with the present to the future. This Wall has been used creatively to link us with other world political struggles. The most impressive of these were:

A rainbow painted through the writing. This, for me, represented alliances with all indigenous peoples engaged in struggles for self-determination, representing 'hope' that we can work together globally against common enemies.

The Wall painted red. It reminded me of those murdered by the forces of the state . . . the blood they unjustly spilt.

Covered in a shroud. This powerful image drew my attention to the invasion of Iraq. How we need to struggle against imperialism.

Visual imagery can impact as strongly as the written word.

Daisy Mules

You're entering a place where everyone has their own rights. It makes me think of Bloody Sunday, the IRA and the RUC.

Aoibheann Gillespie-Mules

It's a political advertising billboard.

Ruadhán Gillespie-Mules

The Palestinian flag flies over Free Derry Wall.

powerful

The medieval City Walls built of stone in the seventeenth century still form the most dominant and powerful historic feature of the city.

Three hundred years later, another wall emerged – much smaller in dimension, but just as powerful in significance. This had been an unremarkable, anonymous gable of a house at the end of a street in the Bogside until, in the late 1960s, it became Speakers' Corner during the civil right protests and marches. During a period in 1969 when the Bogside was a No Go area, local man John 'Caker' Casey painted the words You Are Now Entering Free Derry on it. The rest is history.

It was due for demolition in the 1970s, but wiser heads prevailed and it has been preserved for posterity. Free Derry Corner became an eloquent symbol of resistance to injustice. It has been the location of much tribulation and celebration over the past thirty years – a truly significant landmark.

In Derry, stones do speak. They tell much of its history.

Dr Edward Daly

'If stones could speak'!

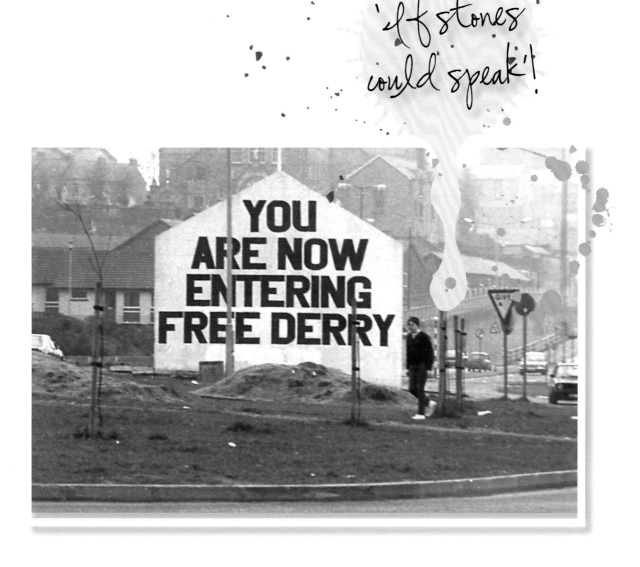

YOU
ARE NOW
ENTERING
FREE DERRY

A crowd gathers at Free Derry Wall for a civil rights meeting (Derry Journal).

37

freedom without the walls

I remember wondering how come they put the road system around what, in spite of its significance, is essentially an old gable wall. In 1967, I'd watched the Housing Trust's redevelopment of the Bogside uproot hundreds of families, demolishing homes and businesses with neither consultation, concern nor understanding for the lives disrupted. My father's piggery had been in Thomas Street. They were refusing to compensate him for the loss of his business, so he refused to go. Eventually, after a protracted eviction process, he won compensation but had lost the community way of life that sustained him. Living in Prince's Street, I lost contact with the Bog, my mother keeping me away from 'over there' as the 'bother' started.

Twenty years on, I was back working with Derry Frontline and The Bogside Sculptors, making theatre and sculpture with the community whose struggle for democracy I'd successfully been closeted from. And as I grew to understand the significance of the Wall, I wondered to myself who had negotiated on its behalf and how come the authorities had listened and moved a whole road system to accommodate it?

Here's what I now know. Willie Hegarty of Wellington Street had got the contract to demolish it, but given its meaning for him and the community, he didn't want to do it. A petition was organised, and while the SDLP felt it should be demolished for safety reasons, Sinn Féin backed the petition's demand to protect it. All I can say now is thanks to all of you.

In the years since '87, the Wall has come to represent for me what I would argue it concretely is – the powerful local symbol of a global aspiration – freedom. And as an artist might analyse a sculpture created to represent this abstract ideal – the appropriateness of the materials and text used, their associations with freedom – it seems worth doing the same with the Wall in a publication such as this.

Firstly, freedom is the entitlement of all of us, regardless of our buying power, so it's appropriate that the Wall began as the gable of a house in a poor district providing shelter for ordinary people. It seems appropriate, too, that the iconic status of the corner emerged with people in the district's awareness that freedom was their entitlement, too. The space at the gable end had become a people's theatre, where questions of freedom and strategies to achieve it were debated, where the will of the community was mustered. In that space, in that time, convention was overturned: anybody could take to the stage and the audience could speak back. And it's appropriate that it was the will of ordinary people that wouldn't let it be demolished. Then Willie's piece of creative destruction, in freeing the Wall from its domestic duties, amplified its significance for the rest of us. The significance is a material connection to what was best in Free Derry: the spirit of people lifted by the need to rely on each other, the creativity this liberates, the humanity it realises.

To that local experiment in democracy had come a text itself internationally associated with freedom. There was a sign proclaiming 'You Are Now Entering Free Berlin' as you entered the American sector of post-Nazi Berlin. It was in this sector, out of cold-war competition to epitomise freedom, that

The Wall is shrouded in black, a memorable protest as US President George Bush and Prime Minister Tony Blair attended an Iraq War summit at Hillsborough in April 2003.

the anti-elitist, anti-authoritarian Free University of Berlin emerged. It became one of the centres of student protest against the Vietnam War in Europe. And in '68, as part of a wave of American university occupations against the war, University of Berkeley students wrote 'You Are Now Entering Free Berkeley' on their occupied building. Here in Derry, Eamonn McCann saw the graffiti in an article on the protests and suggested it to Caker & Co.

Finally, there's the metaphorical nature of the text. Freedom isn't a static end point, neither for a people nor the individual. Rather, it's a process of always going beyond ourselves to a greater sense of what we are, and responding to that understanding – an eternal process of entering. Such an understanding is reinforced in the changing face of the Wall at crucial or lighthearted

moments and in the ongoing use of its back face to debate and amplify threats to our freedom today.

From all this emerges a crucial final point: legitimacy. Free Derry Wall wasn't commissioned by some authority 'representing us' and designed to depict freedom 'for us' while simultaneously cementing their authority 'over us'. Rather, this symbol of freedom acquired its power organically from ordinary active citizens and every day reacquires it directly from us. This immediacy gives it an inherently democratic legitimacy that officially commissioned symbols of freedom usually lack. So it lives among us free and open, reflecting and amplifying our everyday concerns.

Jim Keys

YOU ARE NOW ENTERING FREE DERRY

British soldiers remove barricade material from near the Wall, 1971.

40

Free the Castlerea Five campaign, 2004 (Charlie McMenamin).

The twenty-fifth anniversary of the Battle of the Bogside, August 1994.

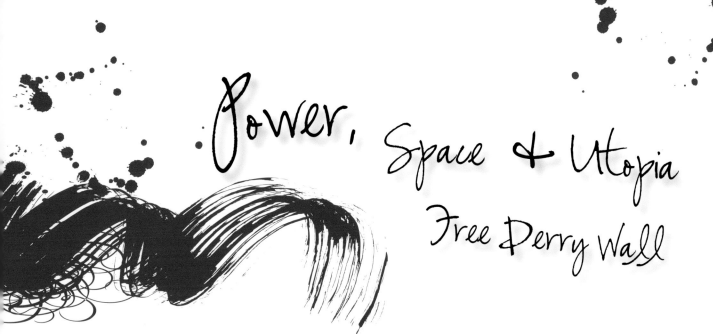

Power, Space & Utopia
Free Derry Wall

Bloody Sunday commemoration, 2005.

D erry belongs to the 'fifth province' of Ireland's mytho-poetic realm: a utopian realm on the edge of the grand narratives of empire, colonialism and statism. And no, we shall never be entirely at one with that other theological promise of forthcoming attractions: nationalism.

The people of Derry are the inheritors of a Great Refusal: 'No'. We shall not belong or conform to a definitive settlement – be it political or cultural. In the order or language, storytelling and signs, the vocation of our people is to disturb, disrupt, question and bring purveyors of 'reality' to account. Experience has taught us that those whose stories, accounts and testimonies count first are people of power: 'realists' are no more than the elites with well-armed imaginations.

But all grand narratives come unstuck in time. One Sunday in Derry, the well-armed imagination of the British Empire State began to unravel before our eyes. The writing has been on the Wall ever since.

Power, Space and Narrative are the currency of our histories and identities. In some spaces, authoritative history is frozen: the war memorial, for example, does not just commemorate, it invents and retells the foundational myth of an imagined community of Britain and a dis-integrating Kingdom. The Bogside Murals have become a sanitised zone for 'tourism': the organised management of boredom.

Traditions are sometimes little more than illusions of permanence. The frozen traditions of yesteryear – even those traditions that once moved us towards liberation yesterday – are the stuff of today's museums.

Other spaces (such as Free Derry Wall) are utopian because they are always contested, always the subject of new stories – sometimes provocative stories about the discontinuities of a city's history of struggle and its bowing of the knee to the arms traders for whom the 'pound of flesh' is no metaphor. Free Derry Wall is a non-place: it is a surfeit of meaning, a mercurial dance of subversion.

If Free Derry Wall is to remain a source of living history in the making – a source of new stories about our freedom, our rights, our humanity and the threats to these things both locally and globally – we must dedicate the Wall to the acts of public speech and storytelling.

Let us create a global stage for all who will come and celebrate our utopian space, not with mere veneration and respect for our local history, but with a New Word, a New Provocation to reflect, to act and break new ground in this city of desire, in this city where to live is to live on the threshold of time (History) and space (Empires of Space).

Free Derry Wall is a Speakers' Corner writ large. Let us continue to liberate and continually reinterpret the Writing on the Wall so that we and future generations can explore, invent and travel to a Free Derry – real and imagined, free and freeing, a message both intimate and distant for our globalised world.

Peter Doran

The Wall is painted in the colours of the Palestinian flag, January 2005.

Anti-Raytheon activists use the Wall as a backdrop to heighten public awareness of their protest against the presence of the multi-national arms manufacturer in the city (Stephen Gargan).

Bandsmen gather at the Wall before a march (Laurie Sparham).

As a kid growing up on the streets of Belfast in 1969 and into the early 1970s, Free Derry Corner and what it represented sparked the imagination and gave the reality to the dream that ordinary people could take on a powerful, tyrannical state and force it to retreat. It represented hope and the power of ordinary people in the face of great adversity.

Féilim Ó hAdhmaill

Hello. My name is José. I'm French. Three years ago I visited Derry and, of course, I saw the Wall. I was proud to see the Irish flag. I like your country and I hope to come back. PS, I got a T-shirt with the Wall!

José, France

Being from Italy, I never had a first-hand experience of the Troubles, thus my support of Irish nationalism was limited and indirect. Last summer, on my fifth visit to Ireland, I went to Derry for the first time. I went to Free Derry Corner and suddenly felt I was finally looking at one of the most important symbols of the Nationalist community. After having read for years about it, I was overwhelmed by emotion in seeing that those few words painted on a wall conveyed all the anger and defiance of a nation which refuses to be buried and forgotten. Free Derry Corner is a national monument and should be preserved as such.

**Jacopo Giorgio,
Roma, Italy**

What does Free Derry Corner mean to me? It means the physical fact and symbol of a community of people in a single place, standing up to declare their freedom against brutality and colonial oppression without the help of the media or the powerful military forces of the world, or the bankers. When I think of the Bogside, I think of Palestine, and I look forward to the day when You Are Now Entering Free Palestine will be a like symbol to cherish.

Tom Leonard

I stand here, and behind me is a small wall with the colours of Palestine painted on it. I look forward to the day when we tear down the apartheid wall in Palestine and build a version of this small wall and write on it, You Are Now Entering Free Palestine.

Dr Jamal Zahalka

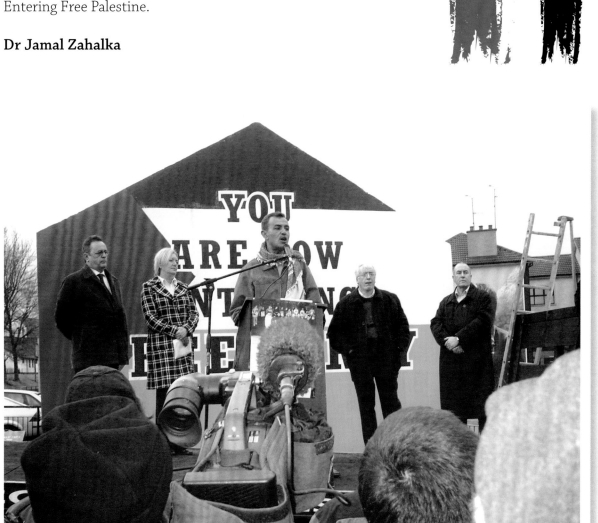

Dr Jamal Zahalka, a Palestinian member of Israel's Knesset, addresses the Bloody Sunday rally in 2005.

Palestinian flag flies at half-mast following the death of Yasser Arafat, 2004 (Adrian Kerr).

Members of the Rossport 5 along with Sinn Féin representatives. L–R: Gerry MacLochlainn, Vincent McGrath, Martin McGuinness, Mary Corduff, Martina Anderson and Willie Corduff (Charlie McMenamin).

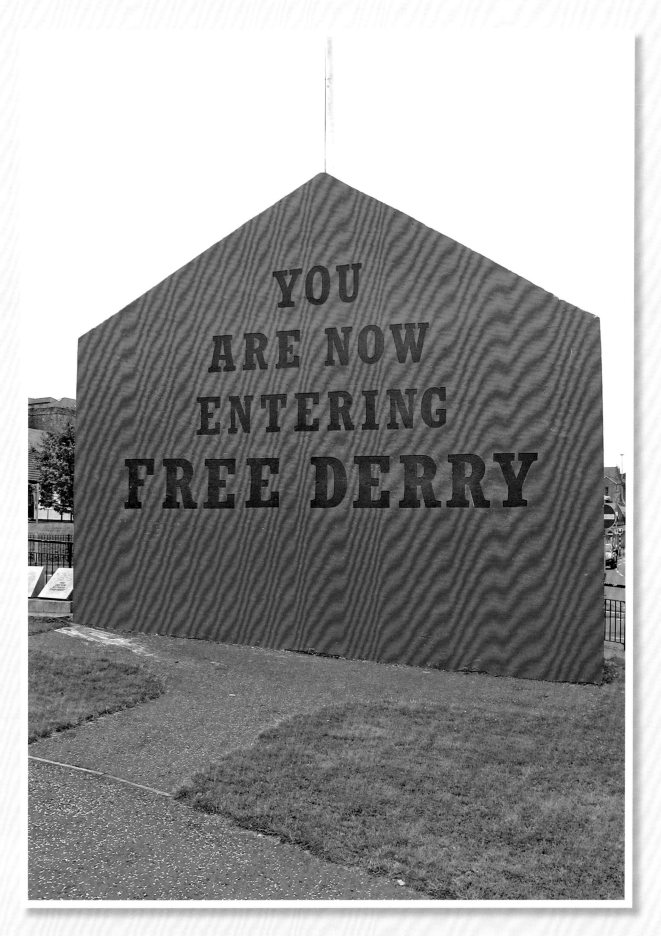

Support for the Gay Pride Festival, August 2007.

British soldiers shelter from rioters with their backs to the Wall (Barney McMonagle).

The Wall remains standing as all around is torn down for redevelopment, 1975 (John McKane).

I remember writing about Free Derry Corner in an article and felt proud to tell people about it despite never having met Caker Casey or even being alive when it came into being. One of its special powers is that its image gets taken away and continues to inspire in books, television programmes, art galleries and photo albums across the world. The reception of art in society is very hard to qualify and quantify, but this book will be a big help.

Whereas the Giant's Causeway attracts visitors in dribs and drabs in tune with Dr Johnson's appraisal – worth seeing? yes; but not worth going to see – Free Derry Corner has become one lump of bricks people definitely *do* want to see. As huddles of tourists take holiday snaps on cold winter mornings, it makes you wonder where You Are Now Entering Free's next incarnation will be – Grozny, Hebron, Tikrit?

Guy King

When ninety-six people died at Hillsborough, the police weren't bothered that much. Okay, the victims' families might kick up a fuss, but they were just working-class scum, they wouldn't have the stamina of 'decent' families, they'd soon go away.

They didn't. They battled for years. And every single year, every single battle, proved how loved those victims were.

Similarly, the people of Derry have fought for thirty-seven years to establish the truth behind Bloody Sunday. Free Derry Corner reminds me of that battle. For me, Free Derry Corner, like the Hillsborough Memorial, is a symbol of enduring love.

Jimmy McGovern

'symbol of enduring love'

The area around the Wall was a focal point for many confrontations with the British Army. Above, a Saladin armoured vehicle in 1971 and, below, paratroopers take up position during Bloody Sunday with their commander, Colonel Wilford.

free derry wall?

Compulsorily polite drivers let you cross.
Big Bros care for you.
Smell of chips.
O'Neill's green and white footielicians.
Dog shite, broken buds, smashed harps,
the odd patch of puke; blue,
brown greasy bags. A terrible beauty.
Recycle yourself mucker!

Locals inn and out. The winos' fly under.
My can is the man. That-has-to-go-hey!

Good mourning hey! A long walk,
January cauld silence, uniforms, rain,
flutes, sleet drums, snow.
After the families,
that auld crowd again.
I'll-skip-that. Aye-me-too.
Pints. Happy-Bloody-Sunday.
Tears of black stuff.
Only the beer runs free.
Just the one wall standing.
Three and a roof to go.
'Architects required' Hey!

Koldo Larrea

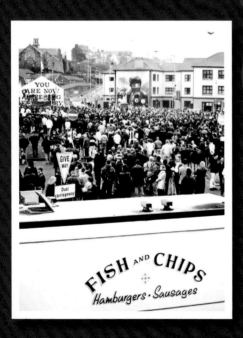

Refreshments at the Wall
(Hugh Gallagher).

Republican rally, 1971 (John McKane).

Bloody Sunday rally, 1984 (Camerawork).

53

Drama group Derry Frontline utilise the Wall to promote their play Threshold, 1992.

The morning the slogan went up on 5 January 1969 – rough, makeshift and defiant, on a grey gable wall – it meant that our backs were against that wall and that we wanted freedom from the cops. Also, from the Unionist Government.

It was echoed during the Battle of Bogside, eight months later, by a slogan on the nearby bookie's shop – We Want Better Odds. And we did: better odds against everything and everyone, including the British Army and Government and the unemployment levels, which remained the same despite all that we had done.

In 1970, when I went to Dublin and joined the Women's Liberation Movement, I saw the slogan differently: it meant that you are now (hopefully) entering a city free from capitalism – but not from male domination.

After internment in 1971, it meant that you are now entering a Fenian city, where men ruled OK.

After Bloody Sunday 1972, it meant that we would not delude ourselves with foreign rule from London – be it capitalist, socialist or liberal – and certainly, never again, rule from Unionist Stormont.

After 1981, it meant rule by Provos only.

After the 1994 IRA ceasefire, it meant joint-rule by London and Dublin.

Now it means whatever the Provos say it means – which, they say, endorses an inclusive world view that is sympathetic to the victims of AIDS and homophobia and male violence against women – as long as the Provos agree with what you say. If they don't agree, forget about free speech. The Provos, let it be said, are not that much different from those who first dreamed up the slogan. All of them truly meant that those who gazed upon it were now entering Free Derry.

Free from what, from whom, for what?

A black ribbon is placed on the Wall by the Pat Finucane Centre to mark the first anniversary of the 1999 killing of solicitor Rosemary Nelson.

Nobody, woman or man, has been really free beyond that gable wall. Derry is not as free a place for women as it is for men. Little thought has been given to that by the (majority on the committee) men who control freedom of expression on the gable wall.

Who is on that committee?

Who even asks the question: what and who are the committee, and how are they, if they are, elected?

You are now entering a Unionist-free, British Government-free, Derry. You are now entering the domain of Derrymen, which is not at all free of the male chauvinist domestic mindset.

Great aspiration, though.

I aspire wholeheartedly to it.

Nell McCafferty

'Great aspiration'

Black-flag procession after the deaths incurred in a SAS ambush at Loughgall, 1987.

Free Derry Corner – a roughly drawn slogan at the corner of Lecky Road and St Columb's Street symbolising the defiance of ordinary people and their desire for equality and civil rights.

A place that provided some of the most enduring images of the Troubles; passionate orators such as John Hume and Bernadette Devlin addressing the crowds; people singing 'we shall overcome'; images of a society in turmoil.

Today, it is a reminder to the people of Derry and of Northern Ireland of the distance we have travelled over the past thirty years and a testimony to the progress achieved by those who worked so long and hard for equality and justice.

Bertie Ahern

Free Derry Corner, for me, symbolises the courage of the people, their hopes for the future and the real spirit of Ireland which will one day – soon – bring unity and peace.

Tony Benn

Lightscape (Dave Mitchell).

YOU ARE NOW ENTERING FREE DERRY

British Army patrol passes the Wall, 1993.

mutual understanding partnership and cohesion

When I was approached to contribute to 'What does Free Derry Corner mean to me?' I felt as a Protestant/Unionist a sense of discomfiture and a desire to renege. However, after a few days of earnest deliberation, I decided to comply with the request.

To me, the Free Derry Corner monument commemorates the events occasioned by the Nationalist/Roman Catholic people of our divided city in heralding our current social and political reforms. The opportunity for greater mutual understanding, partnership and cohesion is now imminent.

Similar to its neighbouring Protestant/Unionist Walker's Memorial, it has local and national recognition as an object of interest to tourists from all over the globe. I wish both of them the respect they deserve as visual symbols in the struggle for equality.

William Temple

Patsy O'Hara Flute Band parade along Rossville Street, 1984, as seen from Rossville Flats.

Above, receiving a makeover as a tourist bus drives by (Dave Mitchell) and, below, Deputy First Minister Martin McGuinness with the organisers of Gay Pride 2007.

Tourists visiting the city view Free Derry Corner in the same way as they view the City Walls or St Columb's Cathedral. It has become a tourist attraction. Most visitors connect Free Derry Corner with the early period of the Troubles in the city. The image of the Wall has been seen in television pictures and newspapers worldwide during the past thirty years and is an important site associated with Derry's recent history.

The Wall has become, as it was during the time of Free Derry, a focal point in the Bogside area along with the murals. 'Free Derry Corner has become a place to be photographed,' as some visitors have said, 'just like the City Walls or St Columb's Cathedral.'

Catherine O'Connor

'place to be photographed'

Sinn Féin's Barney McFadden and Martin McGuinness, 1996 (Jarlath Kearney).

I regard Free Derry Corner as one of the most enduring and seminal images of the Troubles and one of the important landmarks in Derry's modern history. It is a potent symbol of changing times. In the past, it was a focal point for Republican defiance; now, in times of peace, it has become a tourist attraction with thousands of visitors using it as a backdrop for photographs. Free Derry Corner is now recognised as part of the city's history, a place for respect and conservation. I firmly believe that Council, in association with other interested groups, should adopt a co-ordinated approach to ensure that this remarkable site is preserved for future generations and that it becomes one of Ireland's most historic landmarks.

Shaun Gallagher

Spokesperson for the Bogside Residents Group Donncha MacNiallais speaks to the press during the 'marching season', 1996 (Jarlath Kearney).

Three shawled Iraqi women,
Painted on Free Derry Wall
Recall women of the famine,
When shawled Irish women
Faced starvation or emigration
Caused by 'political economy'
This old tyranny
now floats in oil.
Iraqi women watch their
sons face death, torture,
smart bombs
While Irish women, warmed
By central heating
Driving oil-guzzling cars,
Wonder if the offspring
Of our migrant years hear
An Irish echo in the cries
Of the Iraqi women

Bridie Canning

Pride of place, 2007 (Dave Mitchell).

This gable end, solitary, standing alone, a beacon of hope, a loud cry of protest. Its message resonates worldwide. A simple slogan, and a statement of defiance to oppressors the world over. It marked the beginning of the No Go area. A mark of defiance from the people of the Bogside. A refusal to be invaded by British troops – We Shall Overcome, You Are Now Entering Free Derry. It is a symbol of popular resistance and a commitment to support the underprivileged and oppressed throughout the world.

Throughout the period of gerrymandering, discrimination, the housing problems, the riots, the people of Derry rallied together. Clouded in a mist of CS gas, surrounded by barbed wire, bullets, bombs, riots, and state oppression, it stood strong.

Is Free Derry a mindset? Is it the belief that someday We Shall Overcome?

It is bricks, cement and plaster. Its strength lies in its simplicity. It is the people's corner. It is a rallying point in times of community hardship and suffering. Bricks and plaster.

It is a focal point, a local protest point which has become more than bricks and plaster.

Protests and slogans continue to adorn the back of the Wall. Radical causes, both local and international, are addressed from Free Derry Corner. It is a community soapbox, which the community can use to voice its concern and protest on both national and international issues.

But above all else, Free Derry Corner makes a powerful statement: that nobody, whether an individual or an organisation, a dictator or an oppressive government, can ever defeat the Human Spirit, a spirit of resistance to oppression. Spirit can be battered and broken, just like this Wall, but it can and will survive. It can overcome. It is a symbol of hope to all of us who have emerged from the conflict safe. It still stands strong.

You Are Now Entering Free Derry.

We have overcome!

Damian Brown

the bleeding wall

As part of my long but staggered career as a muralist-cum-community decorator, I have had, on numerous occasions, the great pleasure of being involved with projects on, at and around Free Derry Wall, some of which have been detrimental to my own wellbeing. As part of the Gasyard Féile in 1994, to commemorate the Battle of the Bogside, a number of different events and projects were planned. One local artist, Colin Darke, whose excellent work is usually of a political nature, proposed that the Wall should be painted red, in reference to Socialism. The changing of the face of the Wall has always been a very 'tricky' subject – one only ever talked about under the cover of darkness and behind closed doors.

So after hours and hours of meetings, discussions, subgroups and one-to-one dialogue, it was agreed that the face of the Wall could be changed, but with one condition. The Wall would have to be returned to its natural state before the next major gathering, which was the Bloody Sunday march (a time period of almost six months). The project was a great success and people near and far celebrated how well it looked and the statement which was being made. At this point, I would like to add, I took no part in any of these discussions, meetings, subgroups etc. And most importantly, the commitments made to individuals, committees, subgroups etc.

It was almost a full six months later that I became involved in this looming disaster.

Preparations for the Bloody Sunday commemoration were well under way with only a week to go when I was informed the Wall had

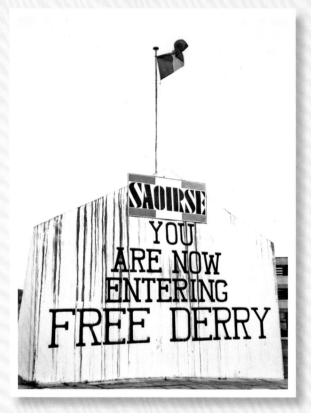

The Bleeding Wall, 1995.

to be restored to it natural state. And in the confusion, I was volunteered to be part of the two-man team that would do the job. First thing Monday morning, myself and local Bogside artist Jim Collins, or Hawks to his very small group of friends, descended on the great Wall of the Bogside to bring an end to what some believed to be the spread of communism in the area. Armed with two rollers, one six-inch brush, two ladders and four litres of matt white emulsion, all kindly donated by a local paint shop, we attacked the Wall. It hadn't rained in two days and things were going well as the last traces of commie red began to fade, overcome by cheap white emulsion. Angry storm clouds filled the Bogside skies and as the first rain drops began the job of undoing four hours' work, we retreated to the warmth of the Bogside Inn to plan the counterattack. Two hours later, the skies clear and the winter sun shining, we returned to find the Wall a roaring red. The only trace of white paint was a large pool of pure white rain water at the foot of the Wall. This time, the paint less watered, we began to cover the unrepentant red. After another four hours and the first coat almost dry, the heavens again fell dark and opened. As the rain ran from the apex down, revealing the red, it looked as if the Wall was bleeding. We stood in shock as the driving rain began to run down the Wall and it slowly began to take on the appearance of a cheap B-movie poster. We retreated in defeat.

The third attempt met with even less success. With no let up in the rain, a last-ditch attempt to save our skin was managed, under extreme weather conditions. We returned the writing to its former black (using gloss paint).

In the run-up to the weekend of events around the Bloody Sunday march, we managed to avoid the committees, subgroups etc, who had been given the reassurance that the Wall would return to its natural state. But thanks to the good old Derry grapevine, we were informed that we were being asked about. We knew that by 4.30 on the coming Sunday, Hawks, myself, twenty thousand people and the world's media would all be looking up at Gerry Adams as he gave one of the most important speeches in Irish history (only speeches of great importance are given from the sacred Wall) and, as a backdrop, Free Derry Wall, covered with what looked like the blood of the dead generations. We were in trouble. A free run in a black-taxi type of trouble.

Every step taken from the Creggan shops on that Sunday was with a heavy heart. By the time we arrived at Rossville Street, Barney was giving out the usual instructions: would such-and-such come to the platform, could the Strabane band stop playing, and would the black taxis assemble at the back of the Wall. As the crowd stood in silence, listening to the names of those

Derry's Walls, so close yet centuries apart, 1995.

murdered being read out, I took cover behind two North Belfast Republicans, waiting to hear my name read out from the platform.

By page fourteen of Adams' very moving speech, I thought it was time to make my exit. As I turned to run, I overheard one of the men in front of me say, 'Jesus, Cruncher, the Wall looks fucking great. That red's to symbolise the blood of the people murdered in Derry.' Then, in unison, whispered, 'The bastards.'

As darkness fell, thousands of Republicans, Nationalists, anarchists and fourteen Socialist Workers returned home by buses, black taxis, cars and foot, their resolve strengthened by the image of the Wall. That image meant different things to all those people. The story of the bleeding Wall is still talked about near and far, long after the words of the great leader have been forgotten.

Needless to say, the Wall was returned to the state in which it was found, and only for the simple reason that the Belfast RTPs (Rough Tuff Provies) thought the paint on the Wall was the work of a genius, permission for execution was denied. But we were later sentenced to a lifetime of committees, subgroups, workshops and flip charts.

If there is a moral to this story, it is that sometimes it is the uncontrollable hand of fate that gives the clearest message, and you can always rely on a North Belfast man for an alibi.

Declan McLaughlin

*The Wall was at the centre of many marches and protests during the decades of the Troubles as, above, in 1981 (AP/RN)
and, below, in 2006 (Charlie McMenamin).*

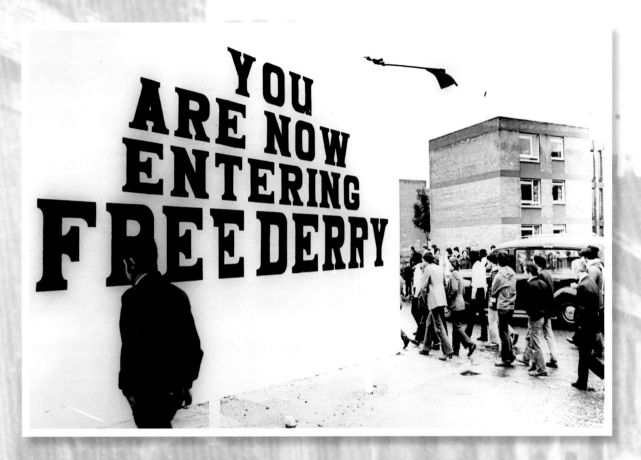

The Wall stands in silent witness to, above, the funeral cortège of Patsy O'Hara, INLA hunger striker who died in May 1981 (Camerawork) and, below, a torchlight procession to mark the beginning of eyewitness evidence to the Bloody Sunday Inquiry in March 2000 (Hugh Gallagher).

Free Derry Wall reminds me of an elderly politician, in the twilight of his years, basking in the new-found respect that age and approaching death demand. The old firebrand, the agitatin' gulpin, is feted and admired, his past indiscretions forgotten, his youthful rebelliousness glossed over, not a bad word to be said about him, not even by his sworn enemies.

From crudity to cultivation, obscenity to measured statement, monochrome scrawl to sophisticated image, Free Derry Wall has matured, much like the ancient politician. And no-one wishes to assault the dead, or those on their deathbed.

Like our corpse-in-waiting, Free Derry Wall is respectable, and has been for years. A delineated spot for protest, a safe area for the gathering of the natives, non-threatening to the interests of the establishment:
'We're angry.'
'Well, get it off your chest, go to Free Derry Wall.' The real message is: 'Who gives a—'

So, what have we got down the Bog? A grizzled old gable wall that has had more surgery, face-lifts, makeovers and image changes than Joan Collins or John Taylor. Is there anything left beneath all those coats of paint, all those slogans? I have a wee suggestion. If you want to preserve a monument, destroy it. Invisible monuments retain a mystique denied existing ones. Shrines and sacred spots are for statues that move, worshippers, and hot-gospellers, not for working people struggling for a better life in a real world.

Seamus Keenan

British soldiers pose in the quiet of early morning for a souvenir photograph in 1988.

Let's be honest. At the time, the Wall may have been like a slap in the face to us, but in twenty years' time, it might be the only thing left to remind us of the Troubles. This is where the Troubles started and it should be retained as a historical monument. I'm sure that soldiers who served in Operation Motorman, for instance, would be glad to go back in years to come and the Wall will be a reminder of that. They may have hated it at the time, but it's part of history now – and you can't deny that.

When people ask me what it was all about, I say how would you like it if you weren't allowed the vote? Or if you voted for a Labour candidate but the election was rigged so that a Conservative always got in? So I think the people were right to go for the vote – of course they were – but it was when the guns came out that it went pear shaped.

Keith
(British Army – from *Derry News*)

you are now entering free derry

For McGuffin

Down Fahan Street
from Butcher's Gate,
There stands some
humble real estate,

its prospects
shadowed by the
walls, And churches
and Memorial Halls.

its front by-passed,
its back bereft,
No roof, Nor door,
Nor windows left;

Last gable of a
cleared slum, That
hosted hooligans and
scum;

or so the lonely
sentinel preached.
Above, the walls
Remain unbreached,

Their clanging London
bells still shout,
'The rich within,
The poor, without',

No walker now, but
still they boast
An army observation
post.

So, who might want
this empty lot? No
church, No party, Owns
the plot.

A movement might
contest the plan,
Some Nationalist
or Republican?

Provisional or
dissident? Or,
God forbid,
The government?

To underline the
Peace Accord,
The Northern ireland
Tourist Board?

No, none of them —
they must be told,
it can't be owned or
bought or sold.

This wall is for
the likes of us, Not
people off a Tourist
bus.

it is the risen people's
voice; At times, to cry,
At times, rejoice.

To trace the precious,
fragile line
From hunger strike
To Palestine.

To testify against
the Peelers And
Homophobes
And weapons dealers;

The British MoD,
of course, And every
other hateful
force,

That keeps us
brutalised and
broken;
'Til Caker's awesome
words are spoken –

Simple yet
revolutionary,
You Are Now Entering
Free Derry.

Robbie McVeigh

Rossville Street, 1983 (Camerawork).

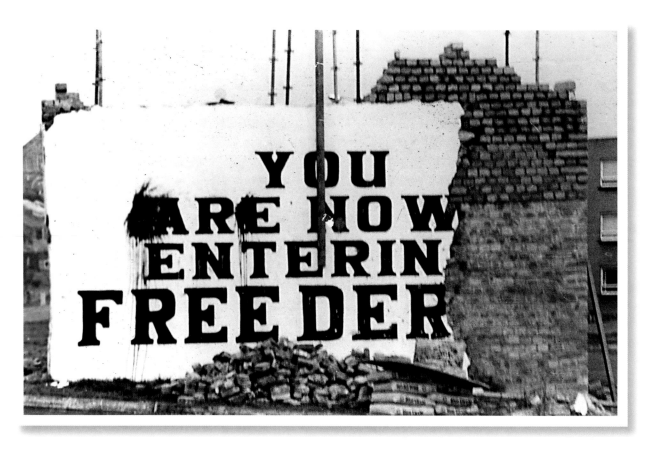

Free Derry Wall under repair after a British armoured vehicle deliberately rammed it in 1982 (Camerawork).

To me the Wall is a reminder of demonstrations.

Demonstrations about civil rights, Bloody Sunday, prison issues, human rights, supergrasses, strip searching, plastic bullets, hunger strikes – I organised some of them and occasionally spoke at them.

The one that stands out in my memory took place on 5 May 1981. The Derry H-Block Committee, of which I was chairperson, would not allow itself to plan a demonstration in the event of Bobby Sands' death. That was an eventuality we could not envisage. When the word came through, people arrived automatically at the Wall, angry, confused, unbelieving.

All the conflicting strands of that intense, ticking-clock, frustrating campaign were present. The people who put their hope in prayer. The people who wanted to attack the RUC and the British Army. The people who believed in peaceful, dignified protest. The relatives of prisoners still on protest. Men and women, the elderly, the young. And despite the late hour, there were many children. I can't remember any well-heeled citizens present. It was a congregation of the poor, the socially and politically excluded.

In contradiction of the often expressed (by me!) secular nature of the campaign, I asked Moya Duffy to say not one, but the full five decades of the rosary. As she led the prayers, the H-Block Committee held a meeting on the best way to protest. We decided, given that our frame of mind was marked by anger and confusion in equal measure, that the most sensible approach was (1) to march there and then to the Guildhall Square and hold a silent twenty-minute sit-down and (2) to assemble the following afternoon at the Wall in a major demonstration. We sat in the Guildhall Square in eerie silence, surrounded by members of the RUC and British Army. We left quietly for our homes.

Kevin McCorry of the NI Civil Rights Association address a rally in 1971 (Eamon Melaugh).

We slept on it. By the time we assembled at the Wall the following day, the penny had dropped. A Western government, loudly proclaiming the ideals of democracy and freedom, had let an elected member of its parliament die on hunger strike for the right to wear his own clothes in prison. A new generation had taken their first lessons in politics. Equality, justice and decency for socially-excluded communities and alienated minorities will not be achieved by seeking intervention from highly placed politicians, clerics, personalities and other 'prominent people' but by forging the strategy, the organisations, the linkages and the means of liberating themselves.

The seeds of a peace process were sown at Free Derry Wall.

Paddy Logue

Hunger strike memorial, 2008.

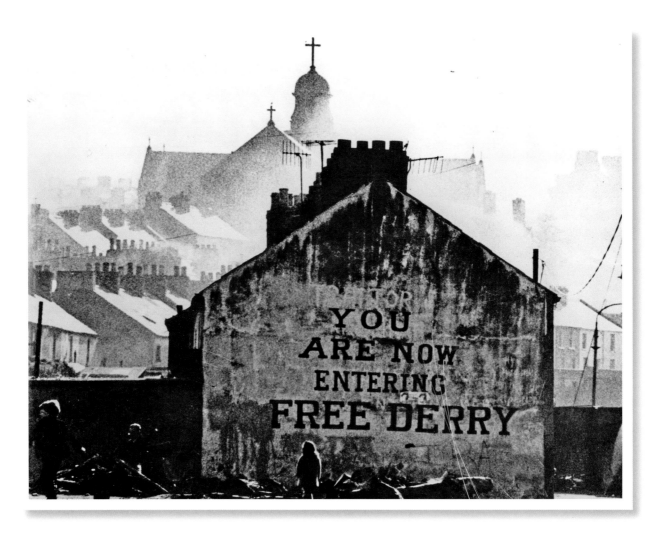

Children playing in front of the Wall, with the Long Tower rising out of the mist in the background.

For me, Free Derry Wall will always be a reminder of the failure of politics, the events that led to Bloody Sunday – a gathering place of remembrance for those killed and injured in the pursuit of civil rights.

It is the place where ordinary people – those who have been excluded, marginalised and demonised – dare to dream that they, too, can have jobs, proper homes and wages, equality and respect.

The people's wall has become an international landmark associated with the ongoing struggle for global social justice and change. It symbolises the right of everyone to work and live in decency without fear and the right to expect a better future.

Conal McFeely

The notion of Free Derry for those brought up in the Six Counties, which was anything but free, caught the imagination of the people of Derry. In simple terms, its message to the Nationalist people of the city was get off your knees, hold up your heads and proclaim, we are Irish, we are first-class citizens, this is our city, this is our place and we claim our rightful place as equal citizens of that place. That's what Free Derry means to me.

But it is also symbolic of a time when a community came together in a spontaneous uprising that sent out a clear signal to the Unionist/British régime that the status quo was no longer an option for them.

Mary Nelis

The Wall when it was merely a gable end in 1971 (Courtesy Frankie McMenamin).

When Jim Collins asked me to write a piece on Free Derry Corner and what it means to me, I had to sit down and think. To me it is probably the most famous wall in Ireland.

I remember going to many marches from Free Derry Wall. Many famous and well-known people spoke at this Wall, like Martin McGuinness, Gerry Adams, Ken Livingstone and others like Barney McFadden and Bernadette McAliskey, one of the Birmingham Six, Johnny Walker, and the one and only Paddy Bogside. Even Vanessa Redgrave, the British film star, gave a talk at Free Derry Corner, the year after Bloody Sunday. I think even John Hume spoke at this corner once.

I have been attending many marches to and from Free Derry Corner since I was a child. I am very proud to say that I knew John Casey, who died just recently, very well. I talked to John many times about the Wall. He once told me that his proudest moment was when he was presented with a gift from Martin McGuinness at Free Derry Wall in front of hundreds of people in recognition of what he had done and which made history all those years ago. There are times when I think John was not fully aware of the lasting impact and significance of Free Derry Wall. I asked John once who his favourite politician was; without having to think, he told me it was Martin McGuinness. Martin was also a very good friend of John's.

Away from the Wall, John was a very ordinary man who lived for his family and would have done anything for them. He lived with his mother, brother and niece, Cathy. Sadly, his mother and brother and John himself all died within a couple of years of each other, leaving Cathy, his niece, who was like a sister to him. She has promised to keep his memory alive.

So Free Derry Wall, what it means to me, is a symbol of resistance and a place where people can exercise free speech and get their message across to not only the people of Derry but to the rest of the world.

Frankie McMenamin

Socialist Environmental Alliance election slogan, 2009 (Adrian Kerr).

'Come a little closer and you will clearly see enough gashes and spots made by vandals: Catholics and other reactionaries, including, of course, Stalinists. These cuts and gashes give even greater life to the frescoes. You have before you not simply a 'painting', an object of passive aesthetic contemplation, but a real, living part of the class struggle.'

Thus Trotsky writing from Mexico in 1938 on the self-defeating sabotage of the murals of Diego Rivera. We have a need of a Trotsky round Free Derry Wall in recent years, who might have persuaded well-meaning curators of history from rendering the gable too meticulously trim.

Trotsky would have a thing or three to say, too, about calls for the Wall to be officially signposted, included with the Tower Museum, Roaring Meg, and the spot where Amelia Earhart landed as a piece of local lore we might lucratively direct tourists to. They are well on the way to making Free Derry Wall into another historic monument, than which there is nothing deader.

The Wall was most alive and appropriately meaningful when it was paint-bombed, pock-marked and chipped at the edges, when its scars were a badge of authenticity, symbol and substance of human experience all around.

It presents itself plausibly now to the world, the letters precisely picked out in conventional font, its coat of paint like a Boss suit draped on proletarian shoulders, neat and clean and well-advised, splendidly isolated from the swirl of humanity, the centrepiece of a Department of the Environment traffic management scheme, its setting professionally landscaped.

We'd be foolish to discount rumour of a lobby for the Wall to be floodlit at night, given the glow of official approval, in the manner of the Verbal Arts Centre, St Eugene's Cathedral, the Civic Offices on the Strand. This would surely be the final, lustreless dignity, making blandly harmonious what was heard in the beginning as a rowdy roar for freedom.

I am reminded that the liberating spirit which Rivera celebrated was eventually compressed and distorted to fit into the party which was to dominate Mexican politics for seventy years, the sweetly named Institutional Revolutionary Party.

Eamonn McCann

Bearing the annual Bloody Sunday ribbon.

Displaying election support for Eamonn McCann with a copy of his 1969 slogan.

Guth na mBan peace camp calling for all-party peace talks after the IRA ceasefire was restored in 1997 (Joe Campbell).

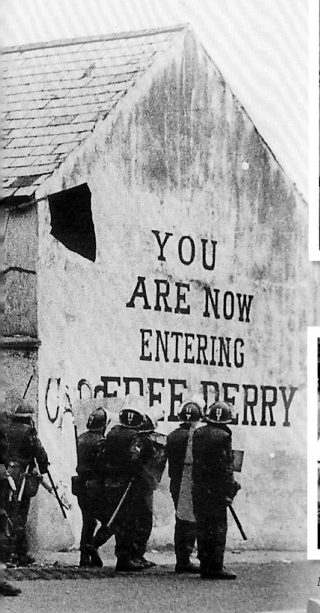

Local Republicans responsible for the maintenance of the Wall (Charlie McMenamin).

L–R: Eamonn McCann, Gerry Kelly, John Tierney and Alex Attwood attend the Bloody Sunday commemoration, 2002 (Hugh Gallagher).

... an ordinary gable wall that lifts the head and heart on each passing

Free Derry Corner to me is Derry's logo: it's the place where politics, history and law intersect, physically and intellectually. It's a monument and a continuing place of struggle. It manages to be both a historic site and a canvas for our hopes for the future. We project onto it both our memories of past campaigns and the demands of our new ones. When friends or visitors come to Derry, it's the first place I take them. To me it is the prime symbol of Derry: despite what some people think, it belongs to no-one other than the people of struggle, the people of change. Long may it stand.

Angela Hegarty

Free Derry Wall is a simple desire of a community's wish to be remembered as they are – free and independent. Derry 'wans' are very proud of it and have passed it on to this Belfast man. In cities around the world, public money has been spent celebrating heroes and achievements; Derry had no such luxury, yet the people left an ordinary gable wall that lifts the head and heart on each passing.

Flair Campbell

The slogan You Are Now Entering Free Derry was painted on a Bogside gable wall the day after police abused residents in the wake of riots which were, in turn, a response to an attack on a civil rights march at Burntollet on 4 January 1969. The slogan caught the mettle of Bogside residents, who threw up barricades and organised vigilantes to replace the police. Now, with the blessing of the planning authorities, the city has another icon, which may be seen to represent that period when the campaign for civil rights for all its citizens is finally being realised. Situated as it is within sight of Derry's Walls, Free Derry Corner can provide a stimulus for viewers who wish to consider both as icons representing opposing loyalties and, in the process, foster mutual understanding.

P O'Brien

I was living in Dublin in January 1969 when the Free Derry slogan was painted. For us, it seemed to articulate the international context of what was happening in the North. The years 1968 and '69 were, literally, revolutionary years, when freedom struggles broke out in a variety of contexts all over the world. The slogan seemed to be saying that Derry's struggle was part of that huge international process. That movement included people in Soviet-dominated eastern Europe, black and coloured people in South Africa and the US, women and gay people all over the world, the homeless in Dublin, as well as many others.

I recall seeing the famous gable for the first time: December 1974. If my memory is correct, the row of houses of which it was the end was still there. It was late at night, so the scene was eerily lit up. For me, the moment was like the first time I saw any of the world's well-known monuments, such as the Eiffel Tower, the Statue of Liberty or the onion domes in Red Square.

Brian Lacey

I remember the original raw scrawl of You Are Now Entering Free Derry and recall the headiness and deadliness of events near and around that Wall.

The dogged humour of the first Free Derry message conveyed a strong spirit of defiance and turning against a bad order. It also expressed hopes for a new and better order. It did not carry the expectation that while the Wall would permanently proclaim its hopeful message, it would also witness hardship, hurt and horror.

Free Derry Corner is now much more than a Derry landmark. It is also more than a partisan prop. It is a place for both remembrance and celebration. Here, people can ponder the abomination of violence. Here, also, we reflect on the freedom values of equality, inclusion, social justice and democracy, which the non-violent civil rights movement stood for.

Mark Durkan

Act of solidarity with citizens of Gaza under Israeli bombardment, January 2009.

Eamonn McCann at the Wall following its transformation by community artists as part of Féile 2007.

Ernie at the Wall. Bert couldn't make it, snowed under, 2007 (Dave Mitchell).

Christmas 2007 saw an unusual visitor to Derry in the form of Ernie the Pez Dispenser. Ernie was originally the property of Anthony Cortese from New Jersey, also known as Snowdog on the photo-sharing online community www.flickr.com. Anthony came up with the idea of sending Ernie around the world to other flickr members who would volunteer to host him for a while, showing him their local sights, then forwarding him on to the next port of call. Before arriving in Ireland, Ernie had been all around the United States and Canada as well as Australia, England, Spain, Germany and the United Arab Emirates.

Local man Dave Mitchell, who uses the name Plastic Jesus on flickr, was delighted to play host to Ernie at the same time as Free Derry Wall had been decorated to coincide with the city's 10,001 Santa charity world-record attempt. Ernie was also lucky enough to experience the festive season with some snow on the ground.

Sadly, Ernie is no longer travelling around the world, having been involved in a tragic accident which saw him being run over by a car on an American Highway. However, the record of his travels remains on flickr at *www.flickr.com/groups/globetrottingernie*.

Above and below, protestors gather at the Wall (Hugh Gallagher).

Aerial photograph showing the crowd in Rossville Street and at Free Derry Wall on Bloody Sunday 1972.

ВЫ
СЕЙЧАС
ПРИБЫВАЕТЕ
В СВОБОДНЫЙ ДЕРР
/ДИСКУССИЯ

free derry wall
multimedia
projection:

The Wall goes international and interactive in 2006 (Ciarán Ó Dochartaigh).

Free Derry Wall was well established as a political landmark when I first began to notice it from my granny's house at 48 Glenfada Park in the 1980s and early '90s.

I remember daydreaming at the window, curious as to how part of the house could stand there. But even then, I am sure I knew what the Free Derry slogan represented.

I remember seeing the Wall transformed occasionally with black-and-white splashes from paint bombs. I couldn't work out who would have the nerve to do this until my father said that the army did it under the cover of darkness. Even so, the Wall was always painted back to its original glory.

This I could comprehend, but one day it was painted red and yellow. It completely threw me, and I am not sure whether I agreed with this blatant change at the time. I think I preferred the familiar black-and-white setting. Whether I agreed or not, it challenged me to accept new things and to consider why it was painted like this.

Free Derry Wall was always at the back of my mind from those early days and through Art College in Belfast and back to Derry again.

I had come very close to making a performance piece there on Bloody Sunday 2002, which I thankfully abandoned.

In 2006, I had the opportunity to make a contribution to the by then long-established artists' relationship with the Wall.

I had permission to make a multimedia projection onto the prepared whitewashed wall, removing traces of the slogan. Translations of the slogan were then projected back onto the Wall including Irish, Polish, Basque, French and the original English slogan. Live electronic text messages and email messages were then projected onto the Wall, submitted by the public, from a live website email and mobile number. One of the key aims was to offer free speech to all on Free Derry Wall.

I hope this piece challenged people to reconsider the Wall the way Colin Darke's piece challenged me over ten years earlier.

Free Derry Wall has had a lasting impression on me. I find the Wall exceptional as a political and cultural landmark, or even public sculpture, that has stood the test of time.

Ciarán Ó Dochartaigh

British troops preparing for a confrontation
with youths in the shadow of Free Derry Wall.

Above and below, Bogside residents vote to remove the No Go area barricades, October 1969 (George Sweeney).

For forty years, the simple words You Are Now Entering Free Derry have been an inspiration to people everywhere in the world that it is possible and necessary to stand up to and defeat oppression. The site will remain a symbol of the struggle for freedom.

Ken Livingstone

The gable wall to me is a symbol of the past and the future. The side that supported the sub-standard housing squeezed between it and McKeown's Lane reminds me of the bad old days when the downtrodden Nationalist people of this area were looked upon and treated as second-class citizens by the Unionist-controlled Corporation. The other side of this erect, proud and defiant monument reminds me of the struggle the people of the Bogside endured to become proper citizens of their own city. It is also a stark reminder to future generations that the bad old days must never be allowed to return.

Neil Campbell

Veteran Republicans Gerry 'The Bird' Doherty and Johnny Coyle (Camerawork).

It's a reminder of all that was wrong and I would be concerned that it would be used in the future to try and justify the things that happened around the time that Free Derry Corner came into being. That was a time of rioting and people attacking the police – it was the beginning of the Troubles. I would be happy to see it retained as a historical edifice as long as it isn't accompanied with the type of historical revisionism that we have come to expect from some Republicans and Nationalists. If they are going to present it as some sort of symbol of resistance and a reminder of how the young people stood up against the British state and all that kind of Provisional IRA propaganda, then I think most Unionists would prefer to see it bulldozed. If, however, they are going to present both sides and say that this is how Nationalists see it but Unionists see it as a symbol of illegality, of petrol-bombing, shooting and terrorism, then I think most Unionists would be happy to see it retained as a historical monument just like any other.

Gregory Campbell (from *Derry News*)

It symbolises resistance to British rule in Ireland. There is nothing more poignant than Free Derry Corner, because, after all, resistance to British rule erupted there in the Battle of the Bogside. It has always been a focal point for the Republican struggle and it will continue to be so, because the struggle isn't over yet. It's a place I've been to many times over the years, but it's also a place that I continue to go to because the struggle is ongoing and Free Derry Corner is a vital part of that. The GPO in Dublin is a very special place because those men achieved something very significant – the freedom of part of the country. We haven't achieved what we have set out to yet, but there's no doubt that when we are victorious in the future, Free Derry Corner will also be a very special place.

Marion Price (from *Derry News*)

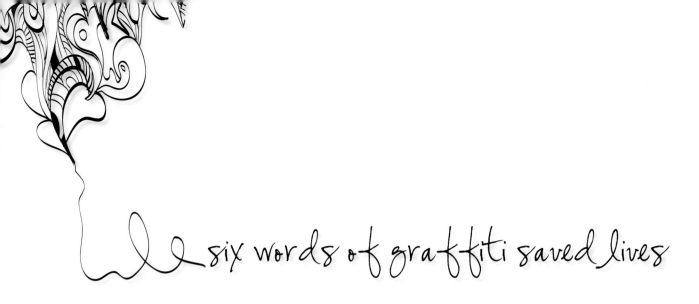

six words of graffiti saved lives

My father came from Bridge Street in the city centre and my mother came from Nelson Street in the Bogside. Myself and two of my sisters were born in Bridge Street before we moved to the Creggan. On many an occasion, I would be sent errands to either Bridge Street or Nelson Street and would normally pass by the gable end of the house at the bottom of Fahan Street that was to become known as Free Derry Corner. It meant nothing to me in those days. People passed it on a daily basis and it meant nothing to them, apart from those who would have leant against it to chat and pass the time of day.

In the event that the six famous words You Are Now Entering Free Derry appeared on that Wall, it became an icon of the Troubles and became famous the world over. When I noticed the writing, it was not just a gable wall anymore: it represented the struggle for civil rights and the quest for freedom for our downtrodden people. It was like knowing someone for years and ignoring them before they became famous.

In the context of Bloody Sunday, Free Derry Corner remains an integral part of the story of that terrible day. Would the story of Bloody Sunday be different if the march organisers had not decided to reroute the march to Free Derry Corner? Bloody Sunday was going to happen no matter what. General Ford had decided to teach the Nationalist people a lesson and had decided to let loose the killing machine of the Parachute Regiment to murder and maim innocent civil

rights marchers. Wilford's animals murdered and maimed with glee, with the knowledge they had a free rein and would be protected by their superiors. The murders on Bloody Sunday were planned. Only for the decision by the march organisers to turn right at William Street and into the Bogside many more could have died or been injured. So by taking that very important decision, they saved the lives of many other innocent people. Free Derry Corner to me is not only a symbol of freedom, but more importantly, it became a lifesaver. People who were there on Bloody Sunday and who decided to listen to the speeches should be thankful for the existence of Free Derry Corner.

Over the past thirty-seven years, the commemoration march has finished at Free Derry Corner, apart from the occasions when we completed our journey to the 1972 march destination at Guildhall Square and once when we stopped at the original army barricade site in William Street. Although we completed our march to Guildhall Square, I will always believe Free Derry Corner is the correct finishing point for our yearly crusade of remembrance for our loved ones, who were cruelly murdered and maimed on that terrible day.

Whether it was Caker Casey or Liam Hillen who painted those famous words on that insignificant gable wall, they should be proud in the knowledge that they saved lives by their six-word graffiti.

John Kelly

*Above and below, crowds gather at Free Derry Wall to remember Bloody Sunday,
mid-'90s (Hugh Gallagher).*

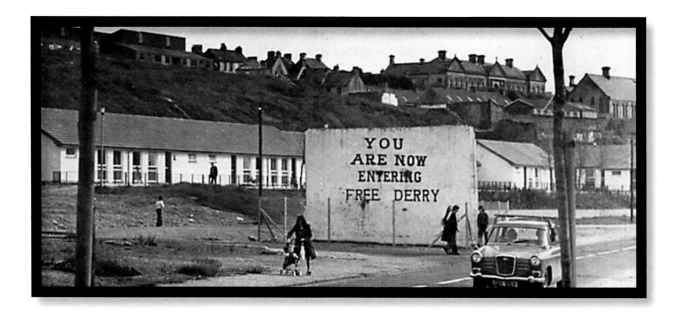

The isolated gable end was a bit shaky in 1975, hence the protective fencing (Willie Carson Collection).

Every community through time and place has the equivalent of a gable wall, a place to lean your back against and dream, a place where children play, young people plot mischief and magic; a wall towards which old men lean for shelter from the wind, to light pipes; against which old women sit to catch the sun, and in whose evening shadow lovers imagine they become invisible.

The hallmark of a sophisticated, advanced and civilised society is a gable wall on which the people also write, draw, paint, poke fun, and protest. Such a wall has no political correctness; it is scribbled on, daubed and dazzled by the multiple contradictory personalities of which it is an expression and an extension. Such a wall is an anarchist, a maverick, full of wit, folk wisdom, foul–mouthed incoherence and irreverence, all competing for a hearing and a vision.

Such a wall is testimony that the people live.

Free Derry Wall was once such a wall. Now it stands alone, majestic in its simplicity but minus the chaotic rhythm of the lives it supported when holding up the row end. It has both a sense of forlorn isolation and triumphant endurance, with its angular glance at the great City Walls above it. It declares with impudence bordering on arrogance that: 'I'm as good a wall as you are, so I am.'

This wall is testimony that the people struggled.

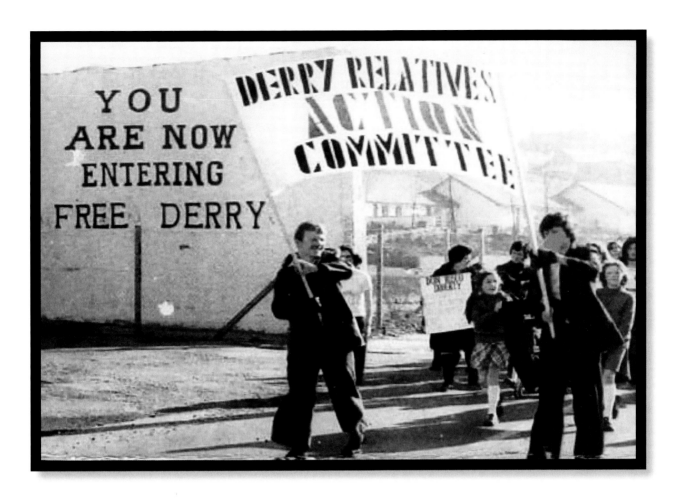

Derry Relatives Action Committee march in support of protesting prisoners, 1980 (AP/RN).

Each time I see it, I am reminded that the perfectly formed and carefully painted black lettering on its pristine white background has what old women long ago would have called a distinctly 'protestant look', a look uncharacteristic of the artistic style of a 'Bogsider'. It would be a foolhardy citizen who would spill an ill-constructed, uninvited sentence on this tableau, now just another war memorial.

In the absence of adjoining walls with which to commune, the other side of the Wall has also long been exposed. By contrast, its face is always changing. The character of controlled expression remains, though Stalin rather than John Wesley springs to mind. This Wall informs the inhabitants of their opinion, lest they forget what it should be.

This Wall probably has a committee, and a long waiting list of opinions to be assessed and appropriately expressed. For all I know, there may well be criteria and quality standards which are applied to the process. One must, perhaps, not only have a message but be able to demonstrate acceptable artistic style, capacity and articulation in expressing it; have access to quality paint and painters (hopefully unionised), and be able to deliver the finished product within a specified time frame, as well as monitor the impact.

Such a wall is testimony to the people's conformity.

The people have no gable wall now on which to lean, write and rail against injustice; no chameleon testimony to continuity, universality, complexity of struggle and life; no room for non-conforming creativity.

Can the people really have nothing left to say?

Bernadette McAliskey

93

I was born in January 1976, around the time that the current version of Free Derry Corner (the stand-alone version) was created following the demolition of the old Lecky Road. As a regular visitor to my mother's relations in the Bog, I have enduring memories of playing around the car park at Lisfannon Park in full view of the 'Corner'.

Fast forward to my two years at St Columb's College in Bishop Street, when I walked past the Wall every morning on my way to school. That was the late 1980s, when the war on the streets had largely become invisible to the naked eye, apart from occasional British Army patrols, Chinook helicopters and the surveillance posts. In essence, the Bog was a place that was safer to walk through than many comparable areas in Britain or the USA, either as a local or as a tourist. Despite this, without publicly declared ceasefires, it was difficult to convince potential visitors that the area was safe to visit, especially due to the negative publicity attached to the area by the British media.

Cue the 1994 ceasefire; what a change of attitude! Visitors flocked to the Wall and the Bloody Sunday memorial, eager to get 'the shot' of them standing in front of a monument which was something to do with the Troubles. By 2001, I was working in the Derry Tourist Office. Very quickly, it dawned on me that a vast number of the people visiting the office weren't looking for the wall on top of the old island of Doire – rather they were seeking the Wall in the Bog, which only confirmed my belief that a visit to the Bogside was now a must for most visitors to Derry.

Two years ago, I took over management of Free Derry Tours, a Social Economy project based in the Gasyard Centre and primarily aimed at telling the real story of what happened in the Bog over the last forty years, while also harnessing the obvious interest in political tourism to generate employment and economic benefit for the area.

A Free Derry Tours group, 2007 (Hugh Gallagher).

For all the guides working for Free Derry Tours there is no better feeling than being able to explain the origins of Free Derry Corner and the events of the last forty years to thousands of tourists and students each year from our own viewpoint, thus exploding the myths and preconceptions that many have about the area and its residents.

One of my key concerns is that the Wall, which is now over one hundred years old, will physically be able to remain standing for another thirty years and more. This obviously raises the issue of whether it should be listed or subject to some other form of preservation order. I know there are differing views on this.

First and foremost, I would hope that the local community members who helped to preserve it every year in the face of British Army and RUC harassment would be among the first to be consulted on its future preservation.

Hopefully, a consensus can be reached which will allow the Wall to be preserved in its original location and form while also ensuring that it receives the care and attention that it deserves.

Mickey Cooper

The Wall with its original 'neighbours' in 1969 (John McKane).

YOU ARE NOW ENTERING FREE DERRY

free the wall free our minds

Get your Free Derry Wall badges, key-rings, fridge magnets, posters, postcards, T-shirts, mirrors, men's handkerchiefs . . . perhaps a plaster model of the said Wall will satisfy your hunger for Free Derry Wall souvenirs? Yours for only £6.99. Whatever next, a free Free Derry Wall soft toy with every McChicken Nugget happy meal?

Maybe the Bogside Artists® should paint Free Derry Wall out and replace it with a black-and-white mural of Free Derry Wall and complete the packaging of the past and pacification of the present. After all, the Wall doesn't make much sense if you're imprisoned by slave wages or long-term unemployment. It may as well read You Are Not Entering Free Derry if you happen to be a member of the travelling community, an ethnic minority or, worse still, female.

The slogan daubed on a Bogside wall forty years ago has served us well, but what about freedom: social, economic and political? It's time to paint the Wall out as a constant reminder of unfinished business.

At the very least, let those who are unseen and unheard scrawl their messages of hope and defiance on this most famed of gables. Failing that, we may as well tumble it. Free the Wall, free our minds.

Jim Collins

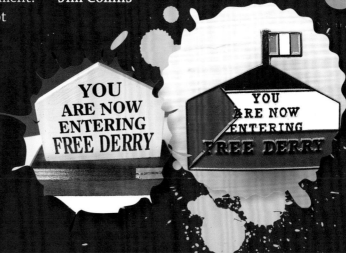

Protest against Israeli settlements in the Occupied Territories, 2007.

'Shoes of the Forgotten' art installation in support of political prisoners, 1995.

my freedom

if someone took away my freedom
My right to pick and choose
i'd go straight to Free Derry Corner
And call the Derry News.

You can be sure you'll not be ignored
Cameramen will come along
with a crowd of people
who'll support and cheer you on.

For it is a voice for freedom
A soapbox to the world
So if someone took away my rights
i know where i'd be heard.

Nastasha de Brún, 14yrs

Catalan solidarity protest, 2007.

'Tent City' demonstration in support of the plight of Palestinians, 2009.

Bogside artist Paul Ruairi, 2008.

He has heard the tin-pig skids,
and the screaming of the lids.

He has seen the young play hopscotch,
while the masked men took pot shots,

against him hands outstretched,
while the innocent got searched,

Snapshots from all over,
damaged by land rover,

Spied on from above,
his colour of the dove,

He wears his tattoo proud,
it stirs the angry crowd,

He watched the thirteen fall,
could do nothing to their call,

This man has seen it all,
his name,

Free Derry Wall.

Paul Ruairi

100

Above and below, Free Derry Wall receives a face-lift (Jarlath Kearney and Hugh Gallagher).

heart of the city

In the Bogside in Derry
there is a Wall,
everyone owns it
yet no-one can call it their own.

The history of the people
stands in black and white,
a statement for employment,
votes and civil rights.

The heart of the city,
the beat that set it free,
I can't believe so many people fought
to give those rights to me.

Kelly de Brún, 16yrs

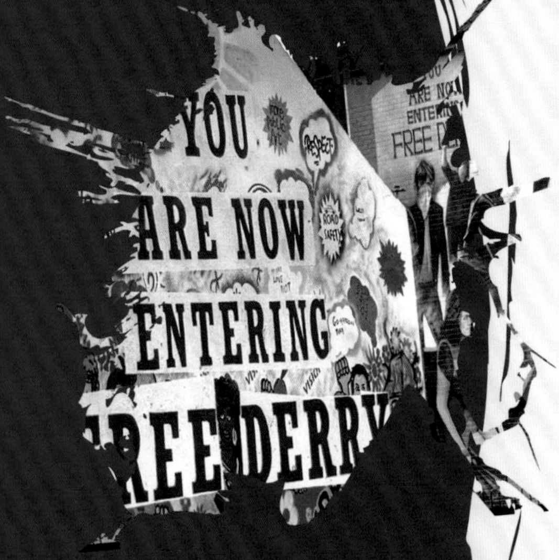

the free derry wall

In the streets of Derry there is a wall,
Free Derry Corner is what it is called.

Every time I see it I think of the Troubles
And how the fight for freedom
Can rise above the rubble.

All of this History,
cemented in stone
shows me the courage
and the hope that lives on.

Jonny Brown, 14yrs

free derry wall

Derry has two famous walls,
one stands big, circular and tall,
the other is a lot smaller
but it means more to me
than the one that is taller.

It tells of freedom
and civil rights,
it reminds me
of what happened
in the Troubles and riots.

Loads of people injured
and lots of people dead
and thoughts of the Wall
bring this into my head.

No one owns the Wall
in the middle of the Bogside,
it's a sign of freedom,
it's a sign of pride.

Seanin Wray, 14yrs

Above from 1995 and below, Bloody Sunday commemoration of 2007.

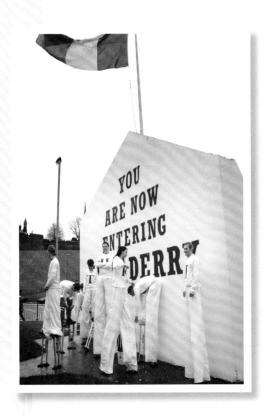

Serene in the snow, 1994 (Stephen Gargan).

The Wall means a lot of things and has different meanings to everyone, but when I see it, I think of the Troubles and the many people who died in the Troubles.

Allan Quigley

The Wall to me means that Derry is free. It reminds me of the Troubles; it reminds me that every person is free in Derry. Sometimes it reminds people about the civil rights marches and the innocent people who were murdered.

When I see the Palestinian flag, it reminds me that their country has been taken over by Israel and their fight for freedom is like ours.

Christopher Lavy

I remember the shock as a teenager of seeing local events in Derry, at the very start of the Troubles, being brought 'into history' by national media coverage and, when the original 'Free Derry' text appeared on an ordinary gable wall, how, for me, it connected directly to images of West Berlin. In that era of the Berlin Wall, huge signs proclaimed You Are Now Entering The American/French/British Zones, and these formed a backdrop for media coverage of student riots which then seemed to be constant in European cities. Suddenly Derry seemed to be part of that. I realise now that Free Derry Wall actually represented a connection between the local and the international in its assertion of defiance and aspiration and a refusal to be written out of history. But we now also know the cost and pain of history being acted out locally, from then on, within sight of that Wall.

YOU ARE NOW ENTERING FREE DERRY

In solidarity with the Palestinian cause, 2005.

105

The fifth corner of the earth? According to Willie and John

It all began with two local characters, Willie and John, who were sitting in the Bogside Inn with their usual pint one Saturday afternoon. John casually asked Willie if he had ever thought of travelling abroad. To everyone's amazement, Willie stood up, braced himself with his arm outstretched holding his pint in the air with a firm grip, and then struck up at the top of his voice, as the whole bar fell silent:

'I had often thought of travelling, the four corners of the earth. What stopped me from going on, was my native place of birth.

'Famous for its landmarks, its culture and its pride. The monumental reminder, the Battle of the Bogside.

'Through blood, sweat and tear gas, we battled to defend. What was once a house on a corner, now stands a gable end.

'Pitch-n-toss and handball, my schooldays I recall. Now a corner with a difference, says the writing on the Wall.

'It has seen all the action, through our Troubles it stood tall. A world-famous attraction, well known to us all.

'Once a war-torn city, a running battleground. It's that Free Derry Corner that keeps me here in town.'

Everyone in the bar responded with rapturous applause. Then, when all was settled, John replied, 'Well, fair play to you, Willie. I'll tell you what, though, that makes us the only planet with five corners!'

Willie sat down, choked with the response from everyone in the bar, and with delight replied, 'Hi, John, you're right. But it's true if you think about it.'

Mickey Feeney

Born into the Bogside in 1968 and growing up in this community has meant that Free Derry Wall is as natural and as central to me as a good night's sleep. It has played, and continues to play, a number of functionary roles that have helped shape and influence me as the person I am today.

Free Derry Wall to me is a meeting point, a platform, a link between the past and the future, a podium, an art gallery, a symbol of resistance, a platform to challenge, a reminder of injustice, a symbol of hope, a gable-end house, a learning curve, an example of community empowerment, a reminder how much still has to be done, an achievement.

Maeve McLaughlin

When pictures of the sign painted on a gable wall in the Bogside, You Are Now Entering Free Derry, began to appear on civil rights marches in London in 1969, it seemed to be too good to be true. For us London-Irish from north and south of the border gathered under the banners, Free Derry represented not only an autonomous Nationalist area of the north of Ireland, but the idea of a new and fair society in the making. Irish feminists like me prayed a secular prayer that 'free' stretched far enough to include women as free and equal citizens, as workers, as wives and as mothers, free to choose when to have their children, and free to choose how many. Forty years on, we know that it was all too good to be true: women in the north of Ireland don't even have the basic right available to most of their European sisters, that is, 'the right to choose'.

Ann Rossiter

"Spoken Word"

Phra
Fra uuuuuuuu deh deh deh deh deh deh
deh
Dehreh dehreh
Deh eeeeeeeee nnnnnn
Nnnga youin youin the ring
Ring ring
Afah afah adah afah adah afah adah
Uuuuuuuuuuu nnnnnn ring deh
Dehree uuuuuuuuuuu oowah rrrrrr
Deh deh ring fah
Entering a fah deh-eh-ree
Deh-eh-ree
You-uuuu
You are now
Entering a free - Derry
You are now entering free Derry
You are now entering free Derry

You are now -
Free Derry. Free, Derry
Was Derry ever free ?
Was Derry ever free ?
Are you free in Derry ?
Are you free in Derry ?
What is free in Derry ?
What is free in Derry ?
Were you ever free in Derry ?

Free Derry free Derry
Was Derry ever free ?
Is Derry free ?
Be Free in Derry
Be Free in Derry
A bah tee yuk a tee bung tay
A bah tee yuk a tee bung tay
Free in Derry free in Derry
Free in Derry free in Derry
Be free in Derry
Be free in Derry

A bah tee yuk a tee bung tay
A bah tee yuk a tee bung tay
Free in Derry free in Derry
Be free in Derry
Evra ung wrung tee yah buk
A tee lung buk
Evra ung wrung tee yah buk
A tee lung buk
Free in Derry
Free in Derry
I'm free
I'm free
In Derry

James King

Protest against President George Bush's visit to Ireland, 2003 (Danny Brown and Frankie McMenamin).

Paul O'Connor of the Pat Finucane Centre addresses a demonstration in support of Palestinians, January 2009 (Charlie McMenamin).

Deputy First Minister Martin McGuinness leads a Sinn Féin press conference on the morning after Mitchel McLaughlin's Bogside home was attacked, 2009 (Charlie McMenamin).

It's a doorstep. They've dug up the surrounding area, they've built roundabouts and plaques at it. They've knocked down the houses around it. It's been photographed by backpackers and tour groups from every conceivable angle. It's been reproduced on grainy black-and-white on T-Shirts. It's been caricatured, symbolised, idealised and criticised. It's been hi-jacked, paint-bombed, repainted and decorated. It's even been replicated in different sizes to take home as your very own. But it's still a doorstep. And it stopped the British Empire.

Joe Duggan

The Wall has always been a place for expressing protest for many issues as above in 2008 (Ronan Moyne) and the target of protest from many quarters, below in 2004 (Adrian Kerr).

freedom's wall

The power to act, speak, or think as one wants without hindrance or restraint

Raising drug awareness.

Highlighting sexism.

Hunger strike anniversary (Hugh Gallagher).

In support of the children of Holy Cross Primary School.

In support of Irish Republicans held in a Colombian prison.

Remembering the 1981 Hunger Strikers, 2008 (Hugh Gallagher).

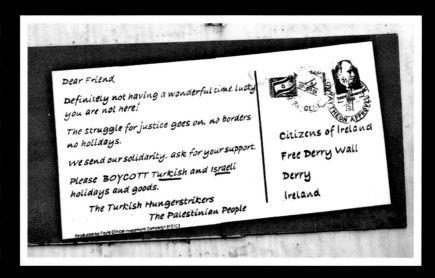

Call for action on Palestine, 2001 (Hugh Gallagher).

Slán Abhaile, a message to the British Army, 2004. Third from right is Caker Casey (Hugh Gallagher).

Bogside and Brandywell Women's Group (Hugh Gallagher).

International Women's Day mural, 1991 (Camerawork).

Call to boycott Israeli goods.

Bloody Sunday commemoration (Hugh Gallagher).

Anti-Raytheon billboard (Stephen Gargan).

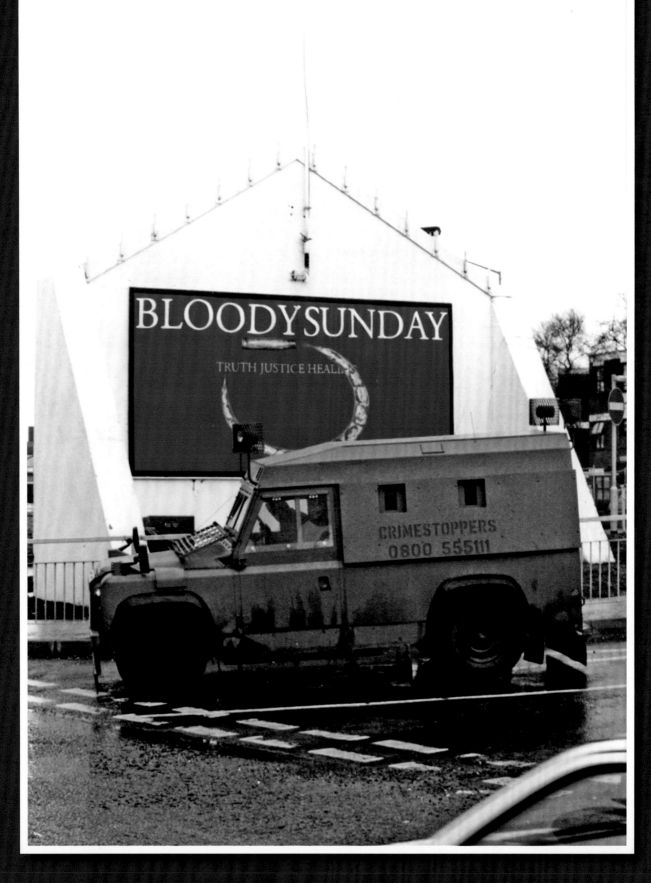

RUC Land Rover passes Bloody Sunday billboard (Hugh Gallagher).

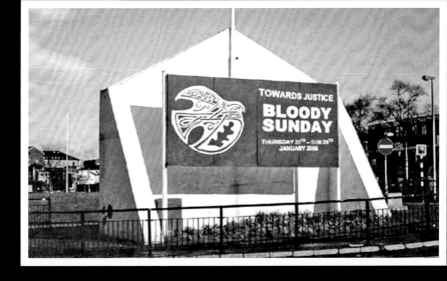

Bloody Sunday remembered, 2006.

Bloody Sunday anniversary, 2002 (Hugh Gallagher).

*Cara Mooney in front of her competition-winning design for the 1987
Bloody Sunday poster.*

Anti-water charges protest, 2007.

Amnesty International mural, 2008.

Anti-Racism Network, 2006.

Support for the nine men who occupied the plant of weapons manufacturer Raytheon in protest against the use of its weapons in the Israeli attacks on Lebanon, 2007 (Dave Mitchell).

Republican Network for Unity mural, 2009 (Hugh Gallagher).

Sinn Féin election mural.

The seventy-fifth anniversary of the Easter Rising, 1991.

Protest against the threatened deportation of Róisín McAliskey.

Call to disband the RUC .

A 'Cher' Guevara image promotes International Women's Day, 2004.

AIDS-awareness mural, 1990. Local man Patrick Doherty, whose father Patrick had been killed on Bloody Sunday, had just died of the disease.

Ballyarnett Travellers mural, 2006.

Bogside and Brandywell Women's Group, 2005 (Hugh Gallagher).

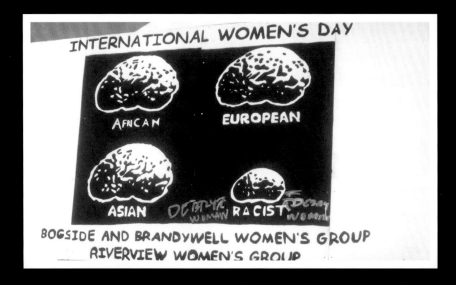

Vandalised International Women's Day mural.

Free the POWs mural, 1995.

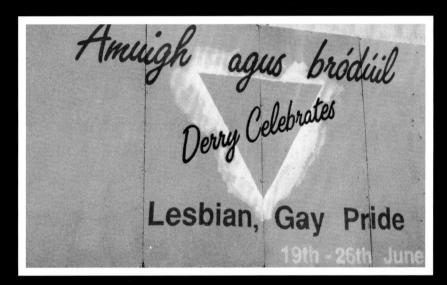

Lesbian and Gay Pride mural, 1993.

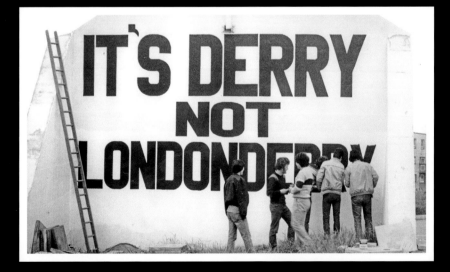

Voicing opinion on the proposed name change of Derry City Council, 1984.

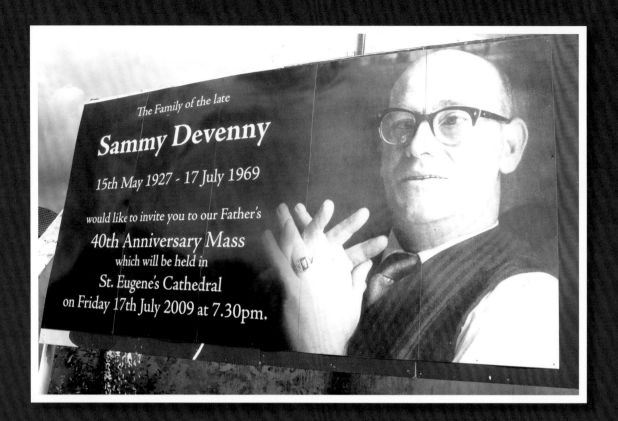

The Family of the late

Sammy Devenny

15th May 1927 - 17 July 1969

would like to invite you to our Father's

40th Anniversary Mass

which will be held in

St. Eugene's Cathedral

on Friday 17th July 2009 at 7.30pm.

*Fortieth-anniversary Mass for Sammy Devenny, the first victim of the Troubles
in Derry, 2009 (Hugh Gallagher).*

Féile billboard, 2002 (Hugh Gallagher).

Call for independent inquiries into the killings of lawyers Pat Finucane and Rosemary Nelson, 1999 (Hugh Gallagher).

Our day will come. Celebrating Derry's GAA Football success with team members Kieran McKeever and Brian McGilligan, 1993.

Christmas-themed Sinn Féin election mural.

Hunger strike anniversary, 1991.

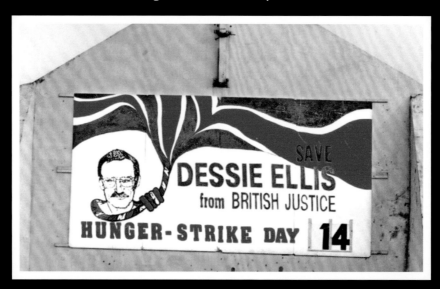

*Mural in support of Dessie Ellis, an Irish prisoner on hunger strike in an
English prison, 1990.*

International Women's Day.

Thirtieth anniversary of the Battle of the Bogside, 1999 (Hugh Gallagher).

First use of the back of the Wall, an Irish translation of the famous slogan, 1983.

Right and above, the Gay Pride mural that was the first ever on the back of the Wall to be vandalised, 2000 (Hugh Gallagher).

Breast cancer awareness mural (Hugh Gallagher).

Sinn Féin election mural (Hugh Gallagher).

Anti-internment mural, 2009 (Hugh Gallagher).

Anti-domestic violence mural (Hugh Gallagher).

Sinn Féin election mural.

Remembering fallen IRA volunteers, 1990.

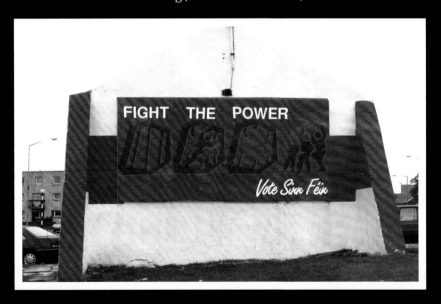

Sinn Féin election mural, 1993.

Suicide-awareness concert, promoted on the Wall in 2009.

Remembering Che, 2007 (Charlie McMenamin).

Security forces collusion protest (Charlie McMenamin).

The Welcome to the Papal Legate mural was subverted to highlight institutionalised Church abuse of children, 2009.

Sinn Féin Youth mural, 2009 (Charlie McMenamin).

Wear an Easter Lily With Pride mural, 2009 (Charlie McMenamin).

The Wall gets a bit of minor surgery (Hugh Gallagher).

Nothing to say today? (Hugh Gallagher).

Caker keeps his hand in (Hugh Gallagher).

Domestic violence awareness mural (Hugh Gallagher).

Promoting Radio Féile, 1999 (Hugh Gallagher).

Call to support the Bill of Rights on International Women's Day, 2007.

Free Derry Corner

Free? Derry Corner, it's not free but it's cheap,
The price that was paid for it would make your skin creep.
And the tragedies and deaths made us all weep,
The anger from troubled times still runs very deep.

Nothing is free, you must pay a price,
Inflation means you must sacrifice
People and places and possessions so nice,
Free Derry Corner's been dear once or twice.

Free Derry Corner, regardless of cost,
The riots and bloodshed and the lives that were lost
Still hang in our memories like an old albatross
But the young of today could not give a toss.

Brenda Brolly

Recreation of Free Derry Wall, to exact size, in the Garden of Hope, Capetown, South Africa, 2006.

Recreation of Free Derry Wall on the set of Jimmy McGovern's 2002 film, Sunday (Stephen Gargan).

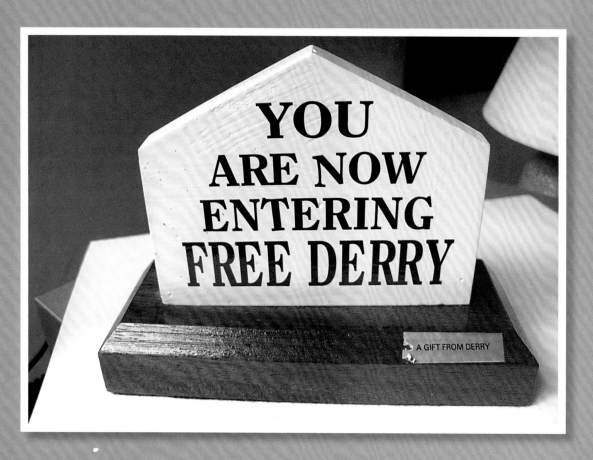

The great Wall made small.

Sinn Féin demonstration, Dublin, 2004.

FÉILE'07ROOTS

Bloody Sunday commemoration
17TH ANNIVERSARY
MARCH & RALLY DERRY
Sun. 29th Jan

SPEAKER:
Martin McGuinness

ASSEMBLE 2.00PM
CREGGAN SHOPS

RALLY AT FREE DERRY CORNER

Above, Féile logo '07, Bloody Sunday march poster, 1989.

Right, top to bottom: Loyalist mural in Bond Street, Derry, showing a Loyalist figure (based on Iron Maiden's Eddie logo) invading the Bogside (Hugh Gallagher); copy of the famous slogan at the end of the Loyalist Sandy Row in Belfast; Féile poster, 1997; Mexico, 2001 (Stephen Gargan); Féile mural, 2004.

Decky McLaughlin's Screaming Bin Lid, 2009.

RUC badge using the Free Derry Wall logo (courtesy Spassy McGilloway).

RUC STRAND ROAD

YOU ARE NOW ENTERING FREE DERRY

LONDONDERRY

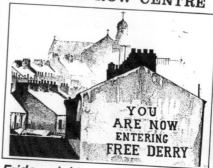

The image of the Wall was used widely in print to promote events and attract the eye (courtesy of the Museum of Free Derry).

Community activist Eamon Melaugh presenting Radio Free Derry in 1969 (Clive Limpkin).

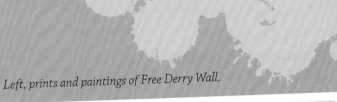

Left, prints and paintings of Free Derry Wall.

You can even stick it on your fridge!

Eamonn Holmes and George Galloway MP take in the atmosphere at Free Derry Wall (Hugh Gallagher).

What's left
Of the concept
Of Free Derry
Corner?
It stands alone
In the middle
Of the road
Fornenst
Traffic
Still displaying
Original words
For tourists' consumption
In contradiction
Of Stormont
And partition.

Dicey

Tourists come from the strangest places to visit
Free Derry Wall (Joe Campbell).

contributors' index

THE MUSEUM OF
FREE DERRY
The National Civil Rights Archive

55 Glenfada Park | Derry | Ireland | BT48 9DR | tel: +44 (28) 7136 0880
www.museumoffreederry.org | info@museumoffreederry.org

**CIVIL RIGHTS • BATTLE OF THE BOGSIDE • INTERNMENT
FREE DERRY • BLOODY SUNDAY • OPERATION MOTORMAN**

"VERY POWERFUL AND EMOTIONAL." – BELFAST

"OVERWHELMING." – USA

"A NOT TOO UNFAMILIAR STORY." – SOUTH AFRICA

"A SHOCKING AND SAD EXPERIENCE." – GERMANY

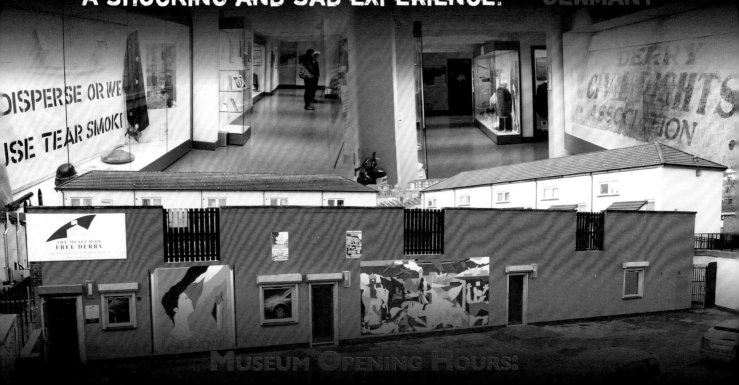

MUSEUM OPENING HOURS:

Monday – Friday (year round) 9.30am – 4.30pm | Saturday (April – Sept) 1.00pm – 4.00pm

Sunday (July – Sept) 1.00pm – 4.00pm. Admission fee applies

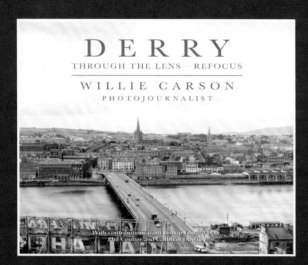
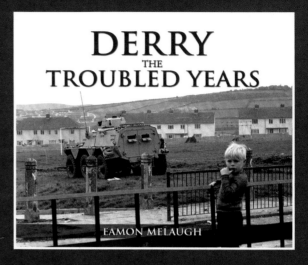
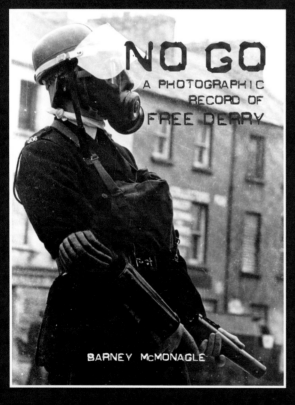
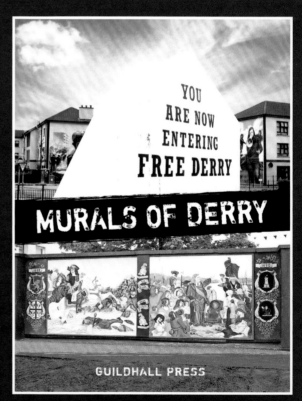